OPERATION CORNWALL
1940 -1944

The Fal, the Helford and D-Day

Loading for D-Day at Trebah Beach *(RCPS)*

Front cover
Falmouth Harbour before D-Day. Naval trot boat in foreground.
Painting by Tony Warren
(B. Lorentzen)

Back cover
The Helford River today - once the setting for secret wartime operations
(Roger MacDonald)

Viv Acton & Derek Carter

OPERATION CORNWALL
1940 -1944

The Fal, the Helford and D-Day

Landfall Publications

First published 1994 by
LANDFALL PUBLICATIONS
Landfall, Penpol, Devoran, Truro, Cornwall TR3 6NW
Telephone 0872-862581

Copyright © Viv Acton Derek Carter

A CIP catalogue record for this book is available from the British Library.

ISBN 1 873443 14 5

Printed by the Troutbeck Press
and bound by R. Booth Ltd, Antron Hill, Mabe, Penryn, Cornwall

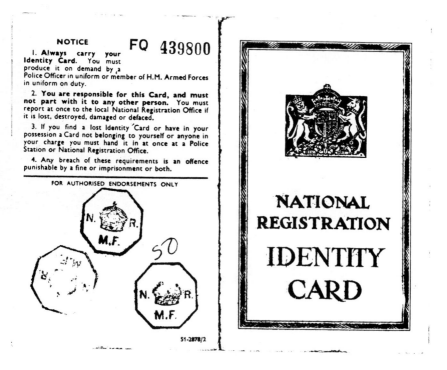

CONTENTS

Don't forget that
walls
have ears!

CARELESS TALK
COSTS LIVES

ACKNOWLEDGEMENTS

We are indebted to many people who have shared their memories and willingly given us help. These include:

Letitia Allen, B.P. Allen, Frank Axford, John Badger, Mary Baker and the BBC, George Benney, Joan and Erling Berntzen, David Brannlund, Dennis Cannicott, Susanne Carter, Monica Cartwright, Tonie Chatterton, Edgar Chinn, J Collier, Mary Collins, Norah and Seymour Cooke, Gwen Coope, Cornish Studies Library, Cornwall Record Office, Jean Crate, Michael Crawford, Graham Crocker, Lilian and Reg Crocker, Archie Curnow, Frank Curnow, DCLI Museum Bodmin, Robert Durbin, Ivor and Iris Dunstan, Tony Eddy, Mick Edwards, Mrs H. Eva, Nigel Eva, Roy Eva, Dan Flunder, Heather Garland and the Mawnan Smith Women's Institute, John Garnett, Peter Gilson and the Royal Cornwall Polytechnic Society, Sue Griffin of Carrick District Council, Charlie Guest, Hazel and Joe Gundry, Cyril Hart, Gina Harrap, Marshall Hellers, Hubert Hicks, Ronald Hitchens, George Hogg and Staff of Falmouth Maritime Museum, Eric Hooper, Imperial War Museum, Irwin Jenkin, Barbara Jenkins and the Falmouth Harbour Master's Office, Valerie Johnson of BP Archives, Ivor Jones, Marjory Jones, Ena Jose, Isobel Kessel, Sylvia King, John Kingsnorth, Bridget Kingston, Tom Long, Wilfred Long, Barbara Lorentzen, Maud Lugg, Ray Lyne, Len Macey, Manaccan History Group, M.K. Matthews of the Helston Folk Museum, Bill Marshall, Donald Miller, Peter Newman, Ann Newton, Hannibal Nicholls, Mary Nicholls, Jean Nunn, Rozanne Oliver, Jack Paget, Harry Pallett, Grace Petterssen, Betty Phillips, Margery Phillips, Clifford Penberth, Melville Peters, Dora Pooley, David and Joyce Rees, Arthur Rendle, Alfred Retchford, Eva Rickard, Maud Rickard, Sir Brooks Richards, Marjorie Roach and the Falmouth Women's Institute, Fire Officer C. Ruberry, Fred Sherrington, Barry Simpson, Mary Steed, Charlie Stevens, Muriel Thomas, Richard Thomas, Charles Thurlow, Tommy Tomblin, Henry Towner, Richard Townsend, Ruth Truscott, Peggy Visick, Barbara Warington Smyth, Nigella Warington Smyth, Peter Waterfield, A.E. Wichelo, Douglas Williams, Women's Royal Voluntary Service - Sue Skelton & Megan Keable, Bruce Wood.

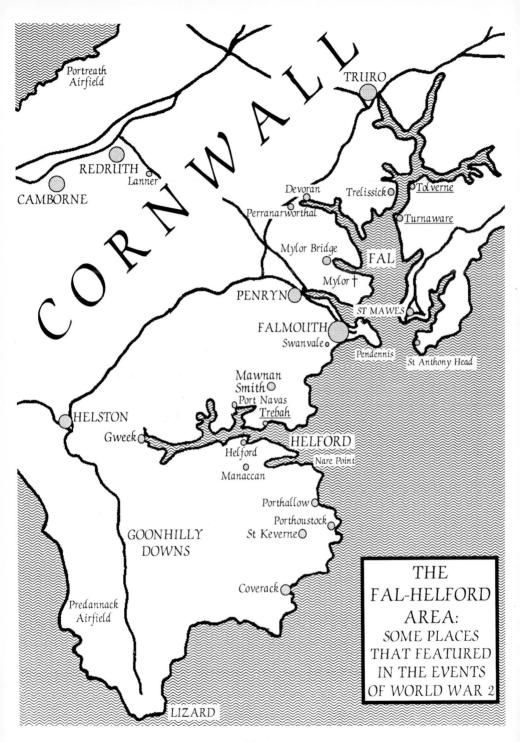

Portreath
Airfield

C O R N W A L L

TRURO

REDRUTH
Lanner
CAMBORNE

Devoran
Perranarworthal
Trelissick
Tolverne
Turnaware

Mylor Bridge
Mylor †
FAL

PENRYN
St Mawes
FALMOUTH
Swanvale
Pendennis
St Anthony Head

Mawnan
Smith
Port Navas
Trebah

HELSTON
Gweek
Helford
HELFORD
Nare Point
Manaccan

Porthallow
Porthoustock
GOONHILLY
DOWNS
St Keverne

Coverack

Predannack
Airfield

LIZARD

THE
FAL-HELFORD
AREA:
SOME PLACES
THAT FEATURED
IN THE EVENTS
OF WORLD WAR 2

INTRODUCTION

"The war robbed me of my youth." "They were the best years of my life." "The war; a terrible time." "People were so much friendlier then. We all pulled together." These diverse views heard during the research for this book indicate some of the problems in trying to give an accurate picture of the war years in Cornwall. If the censorship of the time and the gap of fifty years is added then the difficulties multiply. This is not a comprehensive account, but we hope it will give a flavour of a time which has had such an effect on people for good or ill. "The Second World War in Cornwall? Surely nothing much happened here?" has been another frequent comment. Read this and then judge for yourselves.

Viv Acton
Derek Carter
March 1994

Aerial view of Falmouth from a U-Boat Captain's Manual (H. Towner)

I. THE THREAT OF INVASION

Falmouth Bay was filled with boats large and small. To Letitia Allen and her mother, looking out of the window of their home in Bay View Crescent, it seemed as if so many were crammed into the wide bay, that it would be possible to walk from one boat to another from the horizon to the shore. These were the menacing days of June 1940, when the phoney war had suddenly ended and Western Europe was falling before the might of the German army. Invasion loomed dark on the horizon. Four years later Falmouth Bay was once more to witness the massing of boats on its waters; this time it was for the allied invasion of the German-held Normandy beaches on 6 June 1944, D-Day. But in June 1940 the outlook was bleak.

1. FALMOUTH, THE SAFE HAVEN

In May 1940 the *Falmouth Packet* carried advertisements for "Cornish Riviera Tours" by Taylor's Garage, and "Daily Marine Excursions" to St. Mawes and the Percuil River on the *New Roseland*. On the surface it seemed that there was little direct threat to the way of life of this holiday town on the south coast of Cornwall, but preparations for war had already been made. Laundry vans had been converted to ambulances, government leaflets gave instructions about blackout, food rationing and fire precautions were organised, gas masks were issued and defences for Falmouth Harbour were being set up. There had been more menacing signs of the effects of war: the aircraft carrier, HMS *Courageous*, had been sunk in the Channel, some survivors being brought ashore in Falmouth, and the Docks were busy repairing damaged merchant ships. Britain had been at war for eight months but for most people the time was one of uneasy peace. However this was about to change.

In April the German forces invaded Denmark and then Norway. In May their blitzkrieg attacks continued, but this time moving southwards. Two entries in the Log Book for Clare Terrace School, built on the hill overlooking Falmouth Harbour, illustrate the ominous turn that the war had now taken.

13

"May 10. Education Committee have decided to give a week's holiday at Whitsuntide.

"May 17. The week's holiday mentioned above was cancelled as owing to the invasion of Holland and Belgium by the Germans all schools were ordered to reopen on Tuesday."

The British Expeditionary Force, which had been earlier sent to France, was under great pressure as it was slowly pushed back towards the sea. Major Collier, who now lives near Falmouth, was then a lieutenant in the Royal Engineers fighting a desperate rearguard action, demolishing bridges and trying to hinder the German tanks. In spite of a fierce battle near Arras, which delayed the advance for a short time, the retreat of the allied forces continued. He writes:

"Gradually we moved back carrying out our allotted tasks in the withdrawal along roads which were congested by disorganised remnants of the French army, as well as panic-stricken civilians, men, women and children. We were all subject to frequent bombing raids by German Stukka bombers, which added to the difficulties of movement and caused many delays to our convoy.

"Due to lack of sleep or rest of any kind our drivers, whenever they were obliged to stop, fell fast asleep at the wheel. Indeed this utter exhaustion overcame some drivers while driving and their vehicles ended up against a bombed building or a pile of rubble.

"The view around us was of villages on fire, clouds of black smoke billowing up into the sky, hysterical humanity fleeing to they knew not where, and scrambling into ditches as the Stukka bombers rained down death and destruction. Our Medical Officer continually gave aid and comfort to the wounded, including civilians, some of whom were women in childbirth in the most dreadful circumstances.

"At last we arrived at the approach to La Panne and instructions were received to immobilise all vehicles and render them and any equipment which had to be left behind, useless to the enemy.

"The beach presented a sight of utter devastation, littered with clothing, equipment, smashed boats of every size and description, while to the west, Dunkirk appeared to be on fire beneath a heavy canopy of black smoke.

"I settled my remaining men in the sand dunes to await the possibility of rescue. It came that night, the 1st June, in the shape of a mine sweeper to which we were obliged to wade out and then swim.

"We disembarked at Dover, tired, filthy, unshaven, and with very

SOME THINGS YOU SHOULD KNOW IF WAR SHOULD COME

PUBLIC INFORMATION LEAFLET   NO. 1

YOUR GAS MASK

How to keep it and How to Use it

—

MASKING YOUR WINDOWS

—

EVACUATION WHY AND HOW?

PUBLIC INFORMATION LEAFLET   NO. 3

Read this and keep it carefully. **You may need it.**

Issued from the Lord Privy Seal's Office July, 1939

YOUR FOOD IN WAR-TIME

PUBLIC INFORMATION LEAFLET   NO. 4

Read this and keep it carefully. **You may need it.**

Issued from the Lord Privy Seal's Office July, 1939

mixed feelings, which I cannot describe."

In spite of so many men being saved during these turbulent days, when the sea at least remained calm, there were still 140,000 British troops left in France. More British troops were sent out under Lieutenant-General Alan Brooke to try and reform the BEF, a large number going out through Falmouth, although military security at the time did not allow the publicising of this. But when Paris surrendered to the Germans on 15 June the British forces could do no more. Eight thousand were taken prisoner, but many were able to push their way to Cherbourg and embark, with Rommel's German troops only three miles behind."

This was the time when Falmouth and other ports along the south coast became safe havens as soldiers and civilian refugees packed on to any boats they could find for flight across the Channel. The *Falmouth Packet* on 21 June reports on thousands of troops landing, with men "packed like herrings" on the decks. The article goes on to describe how Falmouth reacted: "people emptied their larders" and bakers provided over 10,000 pounds of bread and 5,500 pasties.

This is borne out by a letter written many years later to the *Packet* by an RAF officer who escaped from further south near St Nazaire.

"I would like to place on record my gratitude to the people of Falmouth for many acts of kindness shown to many men of the armed forces, who limped into Falmouth on the Polish ship, *Sobieski*, one of the last ships to leave France around June 17th-20th 1940. (The Falmouth Harbour Master's Log records its arrival on 18 June)
"Many of us had been "on the run," dodging Jerry for weeks after the fall of Dunkirk. We were a sorry sight on arrival at Falmouth - tired, dirty, unshaven and hungry, and I recall that though we docked after a hair-raising trip, we were confined to the wired-off dockyard until the screening for fifth columnists had been completed.
"Although it is over 35 years since this happened, I remember with pleasure the way in which the Falmouth folk of all ages came to talk to us through the barbed wire and many brought food and drink to keep us going through the long day."

He then mentions three of these people: an elderly lady who brought them a large jug of beer; a gentleman, who drove up in his car and bought up the entire contents of an ice cream barrow for them; and a young boy, who marched along with him when they were allowed out to the railway station, bought him a paper and found him a seat on the train. He added:

"My last full meal had been four days before, and all that we had been able to have on the *Sobieski* was one ship's biscuit and a cup of cocoa. I had been so exhausted from lack of sleep that I had slept on the deck in a coil of rope, oblivious of a dive-bombing attack and a submarine attack outside the Loire Roads.

"I shall always remain most thankful to those good Cornish men and women who sustained our faith in human nature and gave so much of themselves long ago in 1940."

Letitia Allen remembers exhausted soldiers slowly filing out of the Docks until the roads nearby were choked with men. Many desperate for news of friends were questioning each other and swapping photos. They were taken to the Princess Pavilion, the Odeon or the Recreation Ground at the top of Killigrew Street, where many had feet so swollen that their boots had to be cut off them.

Evelyn Radford and her sister Maisie, well-known in Falmouth for their operatic productions, helped deal with this huge influx of people at the Pavilion. Evelyn wrote about it afterwards in the *Cornish Review* and some extracts give a flavour of the atmosphere.

"Wednesday, June 19th. First arrivals, a boatload of survivors from the *Lancastria*, torpedoed on her way home. Men, all sailors and soldiers, blackened and coated with oil. Rush for the canteen, the overflow lying out on the grass in the sun.....They drink very carefully, explaining, 'We've too much oil inside.'

"Thursday, June 20th. Meet last night's arrivals again: all extraordinarily cheery and good-tempered, but many of their stories pretty dreadful......All tell unforgettably of the horror of the crowded roads.......

"A coal boat from Pimpol, with a whole mercantile marine college. Some of them doing their final exam when word came of the Germans close to them. One of the boys heard by chance last boat leaving, and all rushed on board........

"Buses are just coming up from the quay. A crowd suddenly. The advance guard of the 1200 (previously expected), now 1300, subsequently 1600. The last boat out of Bordeaux with passenger room for 300!.....Polish Red Cross, Czech airmen, French and British all services, War Graves Commission, Imperial Airways, Standard Oil Co., Women's Auxiliary drivers, a young woman with several children and twin babies of five weeks.....

"About 3 am a man leans out of the queue: 'You know the man in the hair-net is Baron Rothschild.'.......At 5.30 the stream stops. Step out in the dawn over hundreds lying on the floor, verandah, grass and bandstand.

"Friday, June 21st. The harbour crowded like the Golden Horn, or as M. says, an old-fashioned picture of a naval battle. Tramps, trawlers, sailing boats, liners, naval craft, and all the queer unnameable vessels that the war has brought forth.....

"Saturday, June 22nd. The worst day; rain and hours of waiting for the refugees on the quay. Crews of three torpedoed boats, two British, one Norwegian......All from small craft now, coal boats, cargo boats, trawlers.

"Rest of Days: Sunday to Wednesday. A Belgian cargo boat, wildly over-passengered, a Norwegian trawler, heaps of Bretons, grannies in starched white caps, old men, fishermen in clogs, babies, many without their men, who are joining the fishing fleets. A great reunion of the 'Celtic' fisherfolk!....

"The Belgian liaison man running to know if he can have an order on the canteen to take tea to the Mayor of Antwerp and the Speaker to the Belgian Parliament in the customs."

Eva Rickard came into Falmouth from Helford on one of these days. "It was chock-a-block with people who had come from France. The boats coming over were black with oil and the water was the same. It was frightening. Everybody was scared. There were people lying on the pavement near the Prince of Wales Pier. All the clothes they had were what they wore on their backs. It was sad to see. We fully expected ourselves to be next."

Ena Jose, a Falmouth resident, whose mother was in the WVS (Women's Voluntary Service) which was very active in this emergency, remembers her commenting that although the troops were tired, bedraggled and hungry, they were in amazingly high spirits. This was not true of all of them; some were so depressed that they were throwing or giving away their weapons. The sergeant of Mabe Home Guard gained his Lee Enfield rifle in this way, and the police later had to go round the schools to try and collect those acquired by schoolboys.

Evelyn Radford's account shows the wide range of nationalities pouring into Falmouth, and Wrens working above Taylor's Garage in Fort III, one of the four naval administrative bases established in the town, heard one day the tramp of marching feet, which heralded the arrival of a contingent of the Royal Netherlands Navy. They made a temporary base at Fort III (where Trago Mills is today) before their naval cadet college was

Exhausted soldiers arriving in Falmouth, June 1940 (RCPS)

permanently stationed at Enys House, just outside Penryn, for the duration of the war.

The large numbers of civilians seeking safety in Falmouth was soon increased by refugees from the Channel Islands, who joined the ranks of those fleeing from the German advance and would count themselves lucky if they found space on a boat going to Britain. Ena Jose has an unhappy memory of one such family who fled from Jersey and lived in her house for a time, before they did a moonlight flit, stripping her cupboards bare of her stores of sugar, tea, and dried fruit and leaving an unpleasant mess behind them.

Some refugees stayed for much longer, and on a happier note Falmouth Women's Institute welcomed into their midst a Belgian woman, who five years later was presented with an album of their autographs and a picture of Falmouth, when she was finally able to return to her own country.

Hundreds of refugees flooded into the county, not only to Falmouth. John Jenkin, in a recent article in the *"Old Cornwall"* Magazine has written: "I saw several boatloads come to Newlyn, overloaded with French people and their meagre belongings. A large number of trawlers came from the Belgian fishing ports and fished out of Newlyn for the duration."

But it was to Falmouth, the largest port on the south coast of Cornwall, that most came. Peter Gilson remembers, "From the shore you could not see the horizon, so many boats were packed into the bay; a sight that will probably never be seen again."

Cornwall was also receiving other "refugees" at this time - the evacuees from London and other cities under threat. The county was regarded as one of the safer places in the country, but with the fall of France this was no longer the case, as people were soon to realise. All these refugees must have begun to wonder if they had jumped from the frying pan into the fire. The WVS Quarterly Report for July 1940 explains:

"The first bombs which fell on Cornwall caused consternation.... especially as they arrived very shortly after 20,000 evacuees had come into the County.....WVS has been called out on many occasions to stop panic and calm excitement, particularly in Falmouth, with the arrival of large numbers of refugees from Bordeaux."

Cornwall had entered the war and was now to experience the air attacks that elsewhere had been the prelude to invasion.

2. THE THREAT FROM THE SKIES

"In certain areas the 'warble' of the siren is now a nightly occurrence and is on the whole treated with great calmness." So states the WVS (Women's Voluntary Service) Report for July 1940. Perhaps the use of the word "warble" gives a misleading impression of the repeated rising and falling wail of the air-raid alerts, which in July became only too familiar to people living near Falmouth. The same report highlights a cause for great concern: "There was not at that time an air-raid shelter in the whole of the county."

Cornwall showed that it was very vulnerable now that the French Channel coast was in German hands. About one thousand German bombers and the same number of fighters were based in Northern France and aerial attacks began to be aimed at shipping and ports. Torpoint in East Cornwall suffered first, being so close to Plymouth, but Falmouth was not far behind. The Germans had detailed knowledge of the layout of the harbour, the docks and the petrol storage tanks at Swanvale, as an aerial photo and maps found in their records after the war proved. Their naval

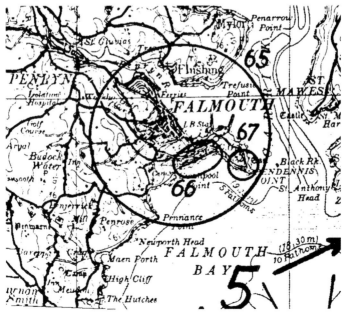

Part of a map from a U-Boat Captain's Manual

ship *Schleswig-Holstein*, which fired the first salvo of the war at Danzig, had made courtesy visits to Falmouth in 1938 and 1939 and on both occasions the men had made good use of the expensive-looking cameras with which they were armed.

During July there were several raids on the town, two of them serious. A letter-writer from Helford described the first raid on 5 July:

"We have come into the War Zone at last. Yesterday afternoon two bombs were dropped on the breakwater at Falmouth, and this morning Helford received its first Air Raid warning. We had a good view of the air battle from here. I came off LDV (Local Defence Volunteer) Patrol at 5 o'clock and went in my field to dig some potatoes and at 6 o'clock a German plane went over and at 20 to 7 the AA guns at Falmouth opened fire and soon there were more planes on the scene. Pieces of shell were whistling past me as I stood in the field."

Falmouth Docks was an obvious target for German planes as it was important for both naval and merchant shipping. It was not easy to hit, being tucked in under the castle promontory, so some bombs probably intended for the docks fell on the town, as happened two days later on 7 July. This was a bad day for Cornwall, because the army camp at Penhale on the north coast was attacked in the early afternoon, with 15 killed and the same number seriously injured and just over three hours later Falmouth had its first fatal casualties.

Ten bombs dropped harmlessly in the water but five fell on the town, killing one entire family and causing extensive damage. The Police War Diary recording this "incident", praises the Dutch seamen who did "splendid work in assisting the demolition squads." Some people had lucky escapes being found alive under the debris of shattered buildings.

The next edition of the *Falmouth Packet* gave some details of this tragedy, naming the killed as, "Mr. George Howard, a retired iron-worker and old age pensioner, his wife, their daughter Mrs. George Pascoe, her husband and their son." One of the lucky ones, in a destroyed house nearby, was a woman from London. Perhaps she had come to Falmouth to escape from danger.

This same edition gave reasons for the need for suppressing information about raids, which could otherwise give valuable help to the enemy. Everyone in the area must have known that another terrible raid had destroyed ships in the docks on 10 July, but no hint of it appeared in the paper. This was the worst raid of the month.

Frank Curnow, who was working in the quarries at St. Keverne further along the coast, had noticed a lone plane high in the sky flying north towards Truro. It was a bright, sunny day and visibility was good. A short time later he saw a plane from the north diving low over the docks dropping bombs. It then skimmed the water roaring away past Porthkerris Cove.

The Police War Diary records what happened:

"At 14.37 enemy plane dropped salvo of bombs on northern arm of Falmouth Docks. The tanker *Tascalusa* was struck and set on fire, the Tanker *British Chancellor* also hit and set on fire. The northern arm was also set alight. Up to 17.00 7 men killed (later amended to 4) and 36 injured some seriously taken to hospital.

"The SS *Tascalusa* is sinking. The fire is being got under control by the Docks and Falmouth Brigades. Total casualties difficult to find on account of number of men working on vessel and pier not yet known."

The Falmouth Fire Brigade record states:

"Several men went afloat to fight the fire from the sea and a total of 17½ hours were put in before any hold could be gained on the fire after 2 ships had been taken away from the wharf. The jetty was also a source of serious trouble."

One of the ships towed away was the *Maria Chandris*, a Greek steamer, whose cargo of cotton had caught alight and was burning furiously.

Ena Jose remembers this attack well as her husband, Harold, was working on board SS *British Chancellor*. "Most of the men with him in the steering flat were killed. He was lucky to escape as he was sitting down; both men standing on either side of him were killed. His dungarees were ripped from shoulder to hem, his shoes were blown off, his face was pitted with hot paint and bits of steel and his hair, eyebrows and lashes burnt off." Jean Crate, one of the ambulance drivers, recalls holding the men's wrists to stop them touching their burned faces as they were rushed off to the hospital.

Ivor Dunstan was working on the Shell tanker SS *Tascalusa*. Pandemonium broke out after the loud explosion. He saw debris flying through the air and the northern breakwater become a mass of flames. Eventually he and others escaped down a rope ladder to a launch which took them safely to Customs House Quay. None of these details appeared

SS "British Chancellor" after the bombing of 10 July 1940 *(British Petroleum Co. PLC & BP Co. Ltd / Kuwait Oil Co. Ltd)*

in the *Packet*. It just recorded a raid on "a south west town," with 4 killed, some injured and some missing.

These constant raids with their tragic results obviously worried people and Ena Jose records a phenomenon also seen in Plymouth and other towns similarly affected.

"When the first bombs dropped on Falmouth people became frightened. I used to stand in the garden of Dracaena Avenue and watch the people leaving the town for the country; God knows where they went......hand carts, bikes, everything was used to carry goods.....For a while Falmouth became a ghost town, people were afraid to venture far and streets and shops were empty."

For children who did not understand the dangers, this could be an exciting time when normal routine went by the board. As the WVS Report shows, there were no air-raid shelters when these attacks began. Arrangements of some sort had to be made in schools, not only in Falmouth itself but also in the surrounding villages.

At Devoran School it was decided that when the Falmouth siren was heard, six miles or so away, the children would file out hand-in-hand, walk through the village to the Old Tram Road, then an unsurfaced track by Restronguet Creek, and hide under the hedge and bushes at Narabo.

Mawnan Smith School, between the Rivers Fal and Helford, had a similar plan. The School Log Book for 8 July 1940 has this entry:

"An Air Raid Practice for the Senior children who were at school was carried out this afternoon. The children were taken to the field below Cock's Close and found shelter against hedges under trees."

This arrangement needed time which was not always available, as the same log book shows two days later when Falmouth had the bad raid on the Docks.

"Surprise air raid about 2.30. The children were all assembled in the 2 lobbies, these being the safest place."

The children were in the lobbies again on the following two days. No doubt the staff were relieved when the summer holidays came. At Falmouth the holidays came earlier than usual. The log book for Clare Terrace School shows something of the turmoil of these days.

"July 8th. The constant air raid warnings since Friday have had such a bad effect on attendance that the Education Committee have decided to close the school for a week.

"July 13th. At the end of the week mentioned above it was arranged that the school remained closed until yesterday - the usual summer holiday."

In August a change of tactics brought night-time raids. A mine sweeper near the Docks was sunk and three tugs damaged. The Police Diary states: "One rating missing - 4 suffering from shock and now in hospital."

But it was the surrounding villages that suffered most at this time, perhaps because Falmouth could not be pin-pointed so easily in the dark. The worst raid was on Gweek, at the head of the Helford Estuary. Margaret Roberts at the Shipwright's Arms in Helford described the attack: "Our fight was at 11.30 at night. 3 planes were over Helford; the row was terrific. One plane dropped 3 bombs at Gweek. One direct hit on a bungalow killed one lady and blew 2 others out of the house. They were unhurt or at least not seriously damaged." Sixty-three-year-old Mrs Loveday Richards was the victim of this raid, and the two "not seriously damaged" were an elderly London couple who had come to see their grandson, an evacuee in the village.

When bombs landed on farmland it was animals that were likely to bear the brunt of the attack. On the night of the Gweek tragedy there were at least five other incidents, mainly south of Truro, in which two sheep and two horses were killed, one cow and two horses had to be destroyed because of their injuries and two foals were injured.

A clue to the reason for this raid on Gweek can be found in another Helford letter written a fortnight later on 24 August, following a bad night when forty-two separate incidents are recorded in the Police Diary.

"Here we had 10 H.E. bombs (high explosive) dropped on Friday night, the first just behind Mrs. Hocking's cottage and the 9 continued in a straight line up to Kestle through the woods. 10 huge holes where they dropped. They made screaming noises like mad seagulls, and on to Manaccan where 22 incendiary bombs dropped. One by the Institute in the Churchyard field, and Mr. Eva's farm.....and various other places. All started fires which were put out. It is a miracle that no one was hurt. They came over every night about 9.30 or 9.45 looking for Falmouth, but we think those on Gweek mistook the River with the tide up, for the Fal."

Bombing was still enough of a new experience for this incident to be mentioned on the eight o'clock news the following day, and for military personnel to come and inspect the craters, measuring them and picking up pieces of shrapnel to gain information on these weapons. The momentum of the Battle of Britain was now building up with the targeting of ports, airfields and factories as Hitler prepared for invasion. Soon a thousand planes a day were sweeping over the country, but then attention was turned on the capital city and the full horror of the blitz began to be felt in London.

On 17 September the forecast for bad weather, linked with the German failure to gain complete control of the air or the Channel, persuaded Hitler to postpone his invasion plans for that year. This did not bring an end to the bombing raids on London and other cities or over the Fal and Helford areas; there were still many more to come and sleep was an impossibility on many nights. Falmouth was to suffer one more very destructive raid before the year ended. The Police War Diary records what happened on 9 October:

"1 H.E. (high explosive) fell near a military camp and failed to explode. 1 fell on Wesleyan Chapel which is used as a hostel for troops. There 3 soldiers and 2 civilians were killed. Chapel not extensively damaged."

The *Falmouth Packet* described the bombs dropped that night as "screaming" bombs as well as incendiaries. It continued, "Despite the imminent danger, the medical and nursing workers kept on with their task in a praiseworthy manner."

The Fire Brigades were also kept busy during these raids. Falmouth town had four brigades during the war. Central Station on the Moor was manned by regulars and had the fire boat crews, but there were also three auxiliary stations, at North Parade, Sea View Road and Gyllyngdune. The last one had bought a Daimler car for £9 and converted it for drawing a trailer pump and later also used a caravan as a mobile canteen, which no doubt brought welcome relief to both fire fighters and victims. In November, members of this team went to London for a time, in an exchange with firemen exhausted by the ravages of the blitz. The Falmouth men had gained early experience in the effects of bomb damage, but they must have been horrified by the devastation in the capital.

The plight of the Londoners resulted in another response, this time from some who had found refuge in the area. The *Falmouth Packet* for 11 October reported, "The Mayor announced that he had received the handsome sum

Gyllyngdune Auxiliary Fire Brigade with converted Daimler *(T. Eddy)*

L.F.B.

Christmas 1940.

Christmas Greetings
and best wishes for the
Coming Year.
From

London Fire Service.

London Fire Brigade Christmas Card to the Gyllyngdune AFS *(T. Eddy)*

of £70 13s from the Dutch Navy in aid of the Lord Mayor's appeal for funds to help the victims of the bombing in London."

Winter, which brought snow and ice, also brought some respite from attack, although the railway line was hit and a train derailed in January 1941, but with the spring came the planes again. Towards the end of March 1941 local people saw the night skies glowing as Plymouth went up in flames; over three hundred people were killed in one night. Jean Crate, driving there the following day, found unexploded bombs beginning to go off all around them as they picked their way through streets only just cleared of rubble for the emergency services.

Falmouth never suffered as badly as this, perhaps because it was a difficult target, and many bombs intended for the docks fell relatively harmlessly in the sea, but people could never escape the constant fear of air raids. Some installed Anderson shelters in their gardens or Morrison shelters in a room, but many made use of what was available, creeping under the stairs or into some other "safe" place. Ray Lyne, who lived on a farm near Manaccan writes, "In the early days we used to shelter by sitting in between the corn ricks and the road hedge but later we stayed indoors and sheltered behind the piano." Some people did not bother and hoped for the best.

The Methodist Church was hit again seven months after its first attack, in May 1941 when three people died and Trevethan School, amongst other places, was so badly damaged that it was later demolished. That evening the audience in St George's Cinema was unaware of the raid because the film, "Waggons Roll by Night," was so loud that it drowned the noise of exploding bombs. It was one of three cinemas in the town and Pat Rickard had gone to the show at the Grand with her boyfriend. On her return to her home in Killigrew St she found her father and brother killed, her mother injured and her home destroyed. Her mother had taken shelter under the stairs and this had saved her life. This tragedy added to the total of deaths for that year, as three people had already been killed in a raid in February in the Park Rise area of the town.

Bad though this was, Penryn suffered even worse. The Police Diary reports:

"0200, 13.5.41, 4 HEs dropped at Penryn. 18 persons killed. 10 seriously injured, 3 slightly. Severe damage to residential property. Road damaged at Quay Hill - local diversion. Damage to telephone system."

Only four months later the Diary records:

29

The Threat from the Skies

"At 22.00 hours 2 Parachute Mines dropped in centre of Penryn Town. One exploded demolishing 6 houses and damaging many others. Casualties 5 seriously injured 16 slightly. One unexploded. 450 evacuated to Rest Centres....Admiralty dealing with unexploded bomb."

Parachute mines had already caused devastation in the area. In March one had landed on the fort on St. Anthony Head on the far side of the Fal Estuary, where officers' quarters, the NAFFI canteen and telephone lines had been badly damaged. Another had been dropped in Falmouth Harbour but had not exploded. Gina Harrap had hitched a lift into Falmouth that afternoon from the farm where she worked at Perranwell and was having tea overlooking the harbour, when she heard a plane and then saw the mine floating down towards the Docks. Before it landed there the wind caught it and wafted it close to Customs House Quay, where it fell into the water.

The log book for Clare Terrace School has this entry for 5 March: "School closed at noon. - not considered safe because of the exploding of the mine in harbour." Attempts were being made to defuse it but with tragic results, as the Police War Diary shows. "Diving to recover parachute mine from Inner Harbour Falmouth, mine exploded. Casualties believed to have been 10 men at work. 2 dead bodies recovered, 2 seriously injured, 2 slightly injured, remainder missing."

Two months later more of these huge mines landed on Mawnan Smith. One completely obliterated a bungalow, killing an elderly couple, and a second severely damaged two houses. The blast broke windows nearly a mile away and the Home Guard man on duty was thrown across the room as he rushed into their headquarters in the Bank. When houses became uninhabitable there was always the unpleasant risk of looters, so the following night the Home Guard had the task of keeping people away. "It was deadly silent and as creepy as hell," recalls George Benney. "A cat crawling across the slates scared the living daylights out of us."

The School Log Book records, "May 9 On arrival this morning I found that considerable damage had been done to the school by the explosion of two German land mines. The lobby roof on the south side was badly damaged and damage was also done to the main roof."

The shorter nights of summer brought some respite, but there were still several incidents as this Helford letter of 14 August shows: "On Monday night 4 bombs fell on Condurrow and Tendera. No one hurt but a cow blown out of the field over the farm buildings and into the farmyard.......stones, slates and debris generally, fell on to the pillow and bed of the expectant mother there who took it all very calmly."

Bomb damage at Mawnan Smith May 1941 (J. Gundry)

But with the autumn came more bad raids. Less than two months after the land mine fell on Penryn, four high explosive bombs dropped in the Gillan area, south of the Helford: "Margaret Roberts' people were killed by a direct hit, and the poor baby died in hospital. All buried at St. Anthony."

About a fortnight later, Mylor had its worst night. Already there had been some damage and slight injuries from high explosive bombs in October, but in the early evening of 13 November four more were dropped right on the village, killing five people.

And so the death toll rose, with five more to be added before the year was out, as a result of further attacks on Falmouth. In some cases the damage was caused by only one or two planes in sneak raids.

In 1942 allied bombing raids on Germany began to increase in ferocity with the first 1,000 bomber raid on Cologne in May 1942. Probably because of this the frequency of German raids in the South-West decreased but when attacks came they seemed to be more intensive. Parts of the historic centre of Exeter were devastated in May as a reprisal for the damage done to the ancient town of Lubeck, and Cornwall also suffered.

Early in the year several attempts were made on Falmouth again, but the difficulty of accurate bombing of the Docks tucked under the headland, as well as an increase in the number of anti-aircraft guns on the hills around, meant that bombs were often ejected off-target. The planes would fly up the Fal Estuary to turn for the run down to the port, and the area of Feock and Restronguet Creek had several incendiary bombs as well as craters caused by high explosives. Sometimes there were other dangers especially in daylight raids. People who lived by the creeks of the Fal can remember bullets being fired as planes flew low over the water, and a letter from Helford describes a similar experience:

"We had an exciting Tip and Run Raid here the other day. Clyde and I were near the stables when suddenly 4 FW-ers came rushing over, machine-gunning. I saw one go close over the roof of the house. I thought it would hit it, and bullets seemed to be flying everywhere from cannon fire."

One couple going off to chapel in Penpol one Sunday evening saw a German plane fly very low up the creek towards them. As they braced themselves for the expected bullets or bomb they received instead a wave from the pilot clearly visible inside.

Firewatching had become an important extra night duty for civilians, with anyone from the age of sixteen to sixty expected to do up to forty-eight hours a week of duty. This proved important in Falmouth, which had a bad night in September 1942, when hundreds of incendiary bombs fell on the town. The fires were soon brought under control and no one was killed, according to the Police Report, but two other places had suffered badly the previous month, Truro and a village on the Lizard.

The Police War Diary gives the bare facts of the Truro raid on 6 August.

"19.25 2 HEs dropped on Truro City. 1 direct hit of Royal Cornwall Infirmary, extensive damage - fire broke out but got under control. Patients evacuated but number trapped under debris. Casualties so far reported, killed 10. Machine and cannon gunning also took place at Railway Station - 2 persons killed. 1 H.E. direct hit on house in residential area - 2 persons killed. Other casualties in town, 100 seriously and slightly injured."

Marjory Jones (née Rule), who was on duty in the officers' ward preparing hot drinks, writes "A thunder of bricks and splintering of glass came almost at the same time as the explosion. I was flung amongst the crockery and saucepans on the floor. Everything was dark. I thought I was buried. Before I became really frightened, however, the falling particles of masonry which made up the thick cloud of dust settled and I saw a square of daylight. It was the light that stopped my fear before it had registered."

One young girl who was in the hospital at the time was Bridget Kingston (née Collins), recovering from meningitis and being visited by her parents that evening. She writes:

"I do not remember hearing any siren or other warning; there was just an enormous explosion.....The blast threw us around the room and when my parents had gathered themselves together after the shock, I was nowhere in sight. My bedclothes and pillow had been blown out of the window and they believed that I had gone with them."

In fact she had been saved from any injury by her mattress, which wrapped itself around her. Her father, who had also escaped unhurt, went off to help in rescue work. However, her ordeal was not yet over. She continues:

"A fire had started and the noise of it was coming nearer and nearer. I couldn't so much as stand by myself let alone walk and I do not know if my mother and aunt could have carried me between them. (They both had been hurt.) Fortunately father returned before they had to try it and as he carried me out, I could see the flames coming from the door of the adjoining room."

Eleven days later it was the turn of a small fishing village. In Bernard Wickstead's book *"Father's Heinkel"*, he describes looking down from a British Beaufighter plane above the Cornish coast after an air raid, in these words, "The Huns had certainly made a mess of it, this pretty, harmless village that had never done anything more warlike than train her sons to be men. Three bombs had hit it and more than thirty houses, three-quarters of the village, were damaged. A cloud of dust, particles of brick and stone, still hung over it like a pall. Ant-like figures in the one and only street were hurrying towards one of the cottages more damaged than the rest."

The village was Coverack on the Lizard Peninsula, and the pilot of Bernard Wickstead's plane was Albert Harvey, who had been born there in the Headland Hotel. They were flying on patrol from Predannack Aerodrome and it was not until he landed that Albert was able to learn that his mother had escaped injury. From the air they could do nothing to help except to search fruitlessly for the planes responsible, but men erecting a nearby radar station at Trelan rushed there at once. Irwin Jenkin had his little, golden cocker spaniel, Ponto, with him, "a good gun dog with a fair nose", and she was soon digging into the pile of rubble. The men worked carefully with their hands to remove the debris but the people were dead.

Four people had been killed and about twenty injured on this day which Cyril Hart, another Coverack man, described in *Cornish Oasis* as, "A beautiful summer's day. A day for going to the beach. A day for going out in the boat. A day for a picnic," until four German planes flew low over the village.

There must be many personal stories of incidents like these; times when people grieved, times of frantic rescue work and times when escape from death seemed miraculous. The threat from the sky was constant during these earlier years of the war and people had to come to terms with it in any way they could. Perhaps seeing some humour in the situation was the best way, as with this story. A farmer went to check on the safety of people nearby, after a stick of bombs had fallen in the area of Restronguet Creek. He became worried when he could not find one man anywhere. Then a couple of shoes sticking out of a haystack showed where his neighbour's instinctive head-first-dive for safety had landed him.

3. DEFENCE AGAINST INVASION

AIR DEFENCE AND DECEPTION

How did Cornwall defend itself against these air attacks which kept alive the fear of invasion? Several methods were used, the most important being the air cover provided by the RAF. St Eval near Newquay was the only operational airfield at the start of the war, as the main attacks had been expected in the east of the country, but with the fall of France imminent the need for Royal Air Force fighter planes in the county became obvious. In the middle of June 1940 Spitfires were flown into the airfield and were soon in action. Dog fights were seen in the sky by watchers below and the Police Diary records "Aircraft heading S.W. chased by British fighters", at the time of the first raid on Falmouth.

With the build-up of German forces across the Channel, bombers flew from here to attack airfields and shipping, the port of Brest being the main target in September when aerial reconnaissance seemed to show the massing of invasion barges. The shortage of operational planes ensured a warm welcome for a flight of French bombers which flew into the base that summer to join the Free French forces.

The strategic importance of Cornwall was now much greater than originally envisaged and during the following year more airfields were built, the most important being at Nancekuke, RAF Portreath, with satellites at Predannack and Trevellas, and St Mawgan became a satellite for St Eval. This increase in air activity meant more fights and damage to planes was frequent. In Truro the firm of HTP Motors went over to repairing aircraft components for Spitfires and the workforce, many of them women and completely inexperienced, soon acquired an expertise that took them out to airfields in mobile units to work on parts too large to transport to the city.

The Police Diary records several of the less happy results of air fights as in March 1941, "British Blenheim Fighter crashed at Goodern Farm, Kea. Machine extensively damaged. 3 occupants safe." The following August it reported: "British Beaufighter crashed into the sea 1/4 S Predannack C.G. Look-out. No trace of machine or occupants."

Barrage balloons were moored near vulnerable places like Falmouth Docks and on the hills around the estuary to deter enemy bombers. The *New Roseland*, which had been advertised for pleasure trips in May 1940,

35

was one of several used as a barrage balloon vessel, but she ended up doing this job in the Bristol Channel. The Police War Diary shows that the balloons could cause unexpected problems as they frequently broke loose from their moorings trailing lengths of dangerous cable. To give just one of many examples: in April 1941 it records, "B.B. broke away, heavy gale. 1 near Punchbowl Inn, cable of electricity line damaged." A few months later it shows that British pilots needed to be just as wary as German airmen: "British Hudson aircraft collided with B.B. cable and exploded in mid-air over Falmouth Docks. One body recovered. Others missing. Machine from 233 Squadron R.A.F. St. Eval."

"As I am writing this, a Jerry is just up over, with the guns firing at him from Falmouth," a Helford man wrote in October 1940. The noise of anti-aircraft guns was increasingly heard with the Royal Artillery based at Pendennis Castle above the Docks and on the far side of the estuary on St. Anthony Head. The Dutch navy also had Bren guns in a boat on the northern arm of the docks and their accurate fire brought down several planes. Other anti-aircraft guns were set up on the routes used by the bombers, as they flew up the Fal Estuary to turn for the run down to the docks.

The Half Moon Battery at Pendennis Castle had been dismantled in 1938 and so had to be hastily re-armed when war broke out, and later in 1942 the defences were improved by building an underground room near the Bay Hotel, where radar information was analysed to be passed on to the battery. This, with the nearby Middle Point Battery, was dismantled after the war, but recently English Heritage has begun to reinstate guns of similar type, although some of the parts have had to come from Germany and Japan, so showing the continued importance of this site four hundred years after Henry VIII's defences were first erected.

The Helford also had its gun defences. Toll Point, for example, at the northern entrance of the estuary, had a Beaufort anti-aircraft gun at the top of the hill, which could fire large shells in quick succession. This was originally manned by the Royal Artillery but later the Home Guard was trained to take over.

Occasionally shells hit the wrong targets. The Police Diary records on 26 November 1940: "AA shell fell in a house in Falmouth. Penetrated the roof and burst inside. No casualties." A few months later a similar incident is reported: ".....at 22.00 an unexploded AA shell penetrated a garage at Four Turnings, Feock. Damage to tools and bench."

There was one way in which everyone could help in the prevention of air attacks. "Being so near to the sea we had to be very sure our lights were perfectly blacked out", so wrote a resident of Durgan. This blackout was put into operation from the first days. Marjory Jones was on holiday from Truro with her parents in September 1939 staying at Hayle Towans. "I went to the window of the chalet and drew the curtain. I was shocked by the absolute darkness outside.....the fact that there were no candles or lamps or electric bulbs flickering across from St Ives assured us without doubt we were at war."

With the night-time raids this precaution became very important so that enemy bombers would have difficulty in pin-pointing their position. Air Raid Wardens would patrol the streets and lanes watching for tell-tale streaks of light, and car lights also had to be masked by shields making night-time driving extremely hazardous. One Helford resident in these war years remembers Mr Oldham the ARP warden "A tall man with a high-pitched squeaky voice and woe betide anyone who showed a chink of light."

Marjory Jones' father became an ARP Warden in Truro. "Moonlight meant danger which in turn meant a patrol along Green Lane with my father. .....because I helped him I had the right to wear a tin helmet. This seemed adequate protection for myself and I thought we were quite adequate as a protection for the whole town against the ravages from Jerry."

There were many cases of people being brought before the magistrates for failing to observe these regulations. Harry Pallett, who then lived at Cowlands Creek on the higher Fal Estuary, was fined 5s for not using lights when he cycled to Carnon Downs in the early mornings. As he writes: "Batteries for lamps were very scarce and even when used the lights were not of much use, as most of the lamp had to be blocked out by inserting a piece of cardboard with only a narrow horizontal slit for the light to penetrate." Perhaps this was a case of officialdom going too far!

But light could be used to lure enemy planes to areas where their bombs would do little damage. This use of decoy sites, or "Q" sites as they were called, to protect ports is not well known, but there were several in the Fal and Helford areas.

Nare Head, to the east of Gerrans Bay and Nare Point east of Gillan, became two "film sets" built with special effects by Ealing Film Studios. Their whole purpose was deception. From the air at night they became a railway system, with lights to simulate signals and the partly-shielded illumination of a railway station. Communications were important objects of air attacks, and Falmouth's rail link with the Docks was vital, so if bombers could be encouraged to drop their loads here, the real station as well as the docks could be protected.

When bombers were detected approaching the area, the lights would be switched on, but only on one of the headlands depending on the direction of the flight path. Aircrew peering through the darkness would observe the signals on lines at the approach to the station, which were really red and green bulbs fitted to vertical posts, then they would notice poorly-screened roof lights of buildings, which in fact were boxes like cold frames with electric light bulbs inside. When they began dropping bombs on to the target, the triangle of lights from doors quickly opening and shutting would be seen. This effect was produced by pairs of tall, rigid frames covered in black felt painted white inside. They were joined together at one end but open about twenty inches at the other end, with a light fixed above switched on and off from the control centre.

This was not the end of the deception. If they dropped high explosive bombs then one or more of the "bomb sets" could be activated. These were fifty gallon tar barrels almost completely sunk into the ground, with flash bags, or electrical detonators, in the bottom and sandbags with cordite placed on the top covered by camouflaged felt. The flash bags were wired up to cables leading back to the control centre.

If incendiary bombs were dropped then the fire troughs could be switched on. There were three of these made of pressed steel about fifteen feet long, twenty inches wide and ten inches deep. They were supported on fire trays with metal legs cemented into the ground and connected by

Nare Point, a decoy site. The "railway line" followed the curve of the path. (D. Carter)

pipes to three tanks, one containing paraffin, one diesel oil and one water. They were filled with combustible material, wood pulp soaked in paraffin, then small kindling, then lengths of dried timber, much of it good quality oak and Oregon pine from the repair yards at the Docks, and then topped by bags of coal and coke. Under all this were regularly spaced flash bags which could be operated from the control centre. The effect would be very realistic, because the paraffin ensured a good blaze, the diesel oil created smoke and the water made clouds of steam as if a locomotive had been destroyed.

The control centre, manned by naval personnel, consisted of two rooms with walls and roof of thick concrete, connected by an entrance hall with a protected doorway and escape hatch. One room housed the electrical generator, a set of lead acid batteries and a fuel supply, and the other was the mess room for the operators, with beds, cooking stove and control panel. At Nare Point this centre was in Lestowder Cliff, close to the present coastal footpath, staffed by Chief Petty Officer Harry Moss and three petty officers, Richard Nicholls, George Pomeroy and Sidney Pender. They worked shifts of forty-eight hours on and twenty-four hours off, and were billeted at nearby Tregildry Guest House and Penare Farm. The men received their orders from Falmouth by an underground cable across the bay, both the sites being under the control of Lieutenant-Commander Dickenson at Fort II, the old Imperial Hotel.

If the site had been activated by a raid or a thunderstorm, then it had to be rebuilt and replenished and the Penryn company of Curtis and Co had this maintenance task. Edgar Chinn, from Treliever Farm near Mabe, would load his father's tractor and trailer on to a naval or Falmouth Transport lorry for use on site to carry materials, such as the 40 gallon drums of fuel, rolls of canvas, bags of coal and cordite from the special locked shed. This job had to been done whatever the weather. "I've been down there at Nare Point, soaking wet and bitter cold," recalls Jack Paget. "We didn't have proper waterproof clothing and what we had, had to be dried in the evening ready for the next day.." They often had to use crow bars and sledge hammers to straighten out the troughs because the heat had been so intense.

The naval party working with them would bring packets of spam sandwiches, tins of condensed milk, packets of tea and bags of sugar. To make their "elevenses" they filled a bucket of water from a stream, and hung it over an open fire until it was black and the water boiling. Two holes were then made with a screwdriver in the tin of milk which was shaken into the bucket, the tea and sugar were then added and the whole mixture stirred with the screwdriver. "I always thought we were in the land of luxury," reminisces Edgar Chinn.

The entry nowadays to the "Q" site control room at Nare Point *(D. Carter)*

The last time that the site at Nare Point needed to be activated was in May 1944, when Falmouth suffered its last and perhaps worst raid of the war. (See "The Last Raid".) By this time the men on the site would have witnessed the waters of Falmouth Bay active with the vessels massing for D-Day, when deception became even more important. Other decoy sites were built to protect embarkation points, on the upper reaches of the Fal and at Frenchman's Creek on the Helford. But in the early years of the war it was the fear of the invasion of Britain, not the hope of an invasion of German-occupied France, that occupied people's minds.

Bomb shelter at Penare built to protect people near the "Q" site (D. Carter)

Issued by the Ministry of Information in co-operation with the War Office
and the Ministry of Home Security.

If the

INVADER

comes

WHAT TO DO — AND HOW TO DO IT

THE Germans threaten to invade Great Britain. If they do so they will be driven out by our Navy, our Army and our Air Force. Yet the ordinary men and women of the civilian population will also have their part to play. Hitler's invasions of Poland, Holland and Belgium were greatly helped by the fact that the civilian population was taken by surprise. They did not know what to do when the moment came. *You must not be taken by surprise.* This leaflet tells you what general line you should take. More detailed instructions will be given you when the danger comes nearer. Meanwhile, read these instructions carefully and be prepared to carry them out.

I

When Holland and Belgium were invaded, the civilian population fled from their homes. They crowded on the roads, in cars, in carts, on bicycles and on foot, and so helped the enemy by preventing their own armies from advancing against the invaders. You must not allow that to happen here. Your first rule, therefore, is :—

(1) IF THE GERMANS COME, BY PARACHUTE, AEROPLANE OR SHIP, YOU MUST REMAIN WHERE YOU ARE. THE ORDER IS " STAY PUT ".

If the Commander in Chief decides that the place where you live must be evacuated, he will tell you when and how to leave. Until you

receive such orders you must remain where you are. If you run away, you will be exposed to far greater danger because you will be machine-gunned from the air as were civilians in Holland and Belgium, and you will also block the roads by which our own armies will advance to turn the Germans out.

II

There is another method which the Germans adopt in their invasion. They make use of the civilian population in order to create confusion and panic. They spread false rumours and issue false instructions. In order to prevent this, you should obey the second rule, which is as follows :—

(2) DO NOT BELIEVE RUMOURS AND DO NOT SPREAD THEM. WHEN YOU RECEIVE AN ORDER, MAKE QUITE SURE THAT IT IS A TRUE ORDER AND NOT A FAKED ORDER. MOST OF YOU KNOW YOUR POLICEMEN AND YOUR A.R.P. WARDENS BY SIGHT, YOU CAN TRUST THEM. IF YOU KEEP YOUR HEADS, YOU CAN ALSO TELL WHETHER A MILITARY OFFICER IS REALLY BRITISH OR ONLY PRETENDING TO BE SO. IF IN DOUBT ASK THE POLICEMAN OR THE A.R.P. WARDEN. USE YOUR COMMON SENSE.

IF THE INVADER COMES

Air attacks on the continent had foreshadowed the advance of the troops on the ground, so what would happen if an invasion fleet arrived off the shores of Cornwall? The threat was greatest during those fine, summer days of 1940 when some people stayed close to their homes fearing the worst. Many had seen the refugees pouring into Falmouth and even more must have heard stories of "the horror of crowded roads" as people fled under attack from the dive-bombers. Would this now be repeated in Cornwall?

At Manaccan, Walter Eva and Miss Trenerry, the headteacher of the village school, made plans to get every child safely home, if there was an invasion during school hours, by using footpaths and fields wherever possible.

Marjory Jones was staying with her aunt in St Mawes.

"Uncle Joe, having heard rumours from everyone, came back one night from the pub carrying lengths of bicycle chains with which he intended to tie us up, Aunt Gertie, my sister Sylvia and myself, before throwing us over the quay. This was to save us from being raped by the invading German army.

"It was not laughable, not then. All night long we waited for the Germans. Came the dawn and time for prayers to be offered. Everyone poured into the church in response to a special appeal which had been made on the wireless for prayers for the army stranded on the beaches of Dunkirk. This was the crucial moment. In the church familiar words rang out with an urgency. Suddenly religion was militant; prayers were spoken as if they were a war chant. We had been reconciled to everything but defeat."

A woman from Mawnan Smith wrote: "It was read out in Church and Chapel that should the enemy make an invasion we were to flee to the fields and not stay at home." Eva Rickard at Helford had a bag packed with a change of clothing hanging on the back of her bedroom door. "What good it would have done I don't know. If there had been an invasion and we had gone to the woods, we would have been bombarded and killed like rabbits." The official Government advice, to encourage people to keep off the roads stated, "STAY PUT." This was in one of the many leaflets produced at this time headed "IF THE INVADER COMES". Roads needed to be kept clear for military movement so civilians were exhorted to "BE READY TO HELP THE MILITARY IN ANY WAY, BUT DO NOT BLOCK

ROADS UNTIL ORDERED TO DO SO BY THE MILITARY OR L.D.V. AUTHORITIES."

Another instruction was to "MAKE SURE THAT NO INVADER WILL BE ABLE TO GET HOLD OF YOUR CARS, PETROL, MAPS OR BICYCLES." In coastal areas boats had to be made unusable by removing oars, sails and engine parts. When Eva Rickard rowed across to Helford Passage on her way to Falmouth, she always left the oars with a friend. Sign posts were taken down all over the country and place names obliterated to make movement difficult for the invaders.

There was a general belief that the first wave of troops in an invasion would come by air, so steps were taken to prevent this by putting stones on possible landing grounds such as Goonhilly Downs, and setting trip wires on long, straight sections of road. These were erected on poles spaced at regular intervals, with the wires stretched from them across the road about twelve feet from the ground, so that vehicles could pass underneath. Some beaches were mined and most were soon bristling with coils of barbed wire and steel girders and planted with "dragons' teeth", as the concrete anti-tank devices were called. Seymour Cooke, who joined the DCLI (Duke of Cornwall's Light Infantry), found himself based for a time in his home area of the Lizard where he helped to construct beach defences. "Our longest run of barbed wire was from Newlyn Harbour to Marazion."

Pill boxes were erected to guard possible landing areas and a constant watch was kept especially along the cliffs and by the roads and railways. The Local Defence Volunteers, or Home Guard as they were soon called, immortalised as "Dad's Army" of television fame, provided many of the patrols on the look-out for invaders or saboteurs. In the early months of the war Susanne Carter, who was a child in Manaccan then, remembers the men of the village enrolling for the LDV at a table outside the village hall. The vicarage had a telephone, not a common possession at this time, and a spare room with its own entrance through French windows which became their headquarters.

The memorial to the Falmouth Home Guard on Pennance Head, south of Swanpool Beach commemorates these men:

".....who during 1940, 41, 42, 43, 44, after their day's work, nightly patrolled this coast armed and vigilant against German landings. Thus they watched 1000 dawns appear across these great waters which form our country's moat."

Once the first scare was over they might well have considered that the most dangerous part of their duty was their transport from Falmouth to the Crag by Maenporth Beach, when they were driven by Wrens in a three-ton

Beach defences at Gyllyngdune Beach & Praa Sands
(T. Chatterton & N. Warington Smyth)

lorry along a narrow, winding road, where trees crowded down to the verge, using the almost non-existent illumination from the shuttered headlights.

What is not so well known is that there was a River Patrol section, which kept watch in the reaches and creeks of the River Fal. Cornwall has the longest coastline of any county in England, so this form of patrol was vital. Every night from the end of August 1940 one boat patrolled the river from Truro down to Turnaware Bar. The patrol had a total of five boats at first, but this was later increased to seven. Ivor Dunstan was on duty on Friday nights when he and his two companions would leave Truro about eight o'clock to go down river as far as Turnaware Bar, and then back to Tolverne where they would spend the night, taking it in turns to be on guard. Mr Newman of Tolverne had lent a room for the men to use every night. Then at about four o'clock they did another patrol to Turnaware and then back to Malpas or Truro, depending on the state of the tide, to arrive at about six or seven o'clock in the morning. They were armed with rifles but never needed to use them against the enemy.

In 1941 they had special praise from General Croft on the occasion when German planes attacked and sank a French vessel laid up in the river near Tolverne in the early hours of 14 April. The River Patrol acted quickly informing the relevant authorities showing that "The River Patrol Organization was functioning properly......We are proud of our River Patrol," said the General.

A resident of the little village of Durgan on the River Helford wrote,

"There was a boom laid across the river; the boats had to go through a certain part to get in or out. ....Our little beaches all along the coast for many miles were all closed to the public. Pill boxes were erected here and there along the cliffs....We had coast watches always on duty day and night.....On the Grebe Beach a system of flame throwers was constructed for use as a defence, and petrol tanks were laid in the woods above the cliffs."

Mines and boom defences were set up in the early months to defend the estuaries. The mines protecting the Helford could be electrically detonated by the naval personnel based in a Nissen hut on Toll Point, who were there throughout the war. Across the mouth of the river, just under the church, was the boom with one gap in it for access which could be illuminated by two searchlights on the lower part of the cliffs. At night two fishing boats, manned by local men, would take it in turns to guard this entrance. Sylvia King, who was a child in Durgan at this time writes, "We had very few toys during the war and would search the beaches for pieces of rubber tubing,

The Fal River Patrol *(RCPS)*

'boom defence parts', which had broken off, because among the kapok in them were rubber balls."

The flame-throwing devices mentioned were not so usual. They were set up where protection was especially important, and the Helford River held secrets which many local people knew little about. During the months of the phoney war the government had built up large stocks of petrol, and the idea of a sea flame barrage was tried out in the Solent and in Studland Bay near Poole during the winter of 1940-41. When it proved successful plans were made to cover fifty miles of the coast with this form of protection. Lack of steel prevented this from being fully implemented but some were built, such as at Porthcurnow, where the transatlantic telecommunications cable came ashore, and on the Helford.

Three large tanks were built into the hillside in Grebe Woods, near the village of Durgan. Pipes led from them down the cliffs to a horizontal jet pipe along the top of the beach. A mixture of petrol and oil could then be pumped down to "spray out across the river like water from a fireman's hose," as John Badger recalls, and when it was ignited for testing "three-quarters of the river from the Grebe to nearly the boom would be alight. Any boat caught in it would have been burnt to a cinder." Joe Gundry remembers that the flames produced intense smoke and heat which scorched the trees nearby.

Although the fear of invasion receded after 1940, it remained a possibility for much longer, so that training was carried out and more elaborate defences were erected. Exercises were held in Falmouth to practise for this eventuality with roads closed off to civilians but as Joan Berntzen (née Belletti), then a young ARP warden, recalls, when she had to direct cars away from these areas she had to be very careful to say, "This is an exercise." The authorities did not want to create panic.

In November 1942 Coverack School had contingency plans for closure if invasion happened and Mawnan Smith School Log Book has this entry for March 1943: "Telephone (test) message just received per Mr James (next door to school) from the District Clerk giving instructions that the school must be closed owing to enemy invasion. The children were formally told but it was made quite clear that message was only a test." This type of exercise would not have been undertaken lightly.

Details about the different types of defences would have been kept very secret but there was always a fear, not only of spies but also of careless talk. "Be like Dad, keep Mum", was one of the many slogans thought up to emphasise the importance of silence, and of course if the worst had happened and the Germans had landed then a Government leaflet instructed:

Do not tell the enemy anything
  Do not give him anything
    Do not help him in any way

What was never told in these leaflets or made public, was that secret armies were being trained to act as resistance fighters if the country were to be invaded.

4. THE SECRET ARMY

"You were invited to do a job which would require more skill and coolness, more hard work and greater danger than was demanded of any other voluntary organisation......It will not be forgotten." So wrote Colonel Douglas, the commander of the Auxiliary Units, when they were being disbanded in November 1944. How many people today have remembered what these men were prepared to do? Their existence was a secret during the war and it was only shortly before the end of the war in Europe that the government announced that these units had been formed.

This secret army was largely the creation of Major Colin Gubbins who had produced in 1939 two pamphlets on guerilla warfare tactics. When invasion of the country seemed imminent, preparations were made for a properly trained body of resistance fighters. It was decided to concentrate resistance units in a coastal strip about thirty miles deep around all the shores of Britain except for those opposite Ireland. This was not to be a centralised organisation but divided into independent groups in each area.

Each Auxiliary Unit (a purposely vague name) consisted of a few hand-picked local men with an intimate knowledge of their own area. They had to be vetted carefully with a full police investigation into their background. Once accepted they underwent training by specially-chosen army officers, in demolition, unarmed combat and the art of moving through the countryside unseen and unheard. Every unit had a well-stocked, well-armed hideout to which it would go if the Germans came and from this base they would creep out to perform their acts of sabotage. They wore the uniform of the Home Guard to give cover for their activities, but they were nowhere officially recognised, so they would not have had the protection of the Geneva Convention afforded to military personnel. The organisation was so secret that their families often had no idea of their involvement.

In Cornwall, by late 1941, there were 195 men divided into 28 patrols. The army officer in charge here was Captain Dingley with his headquarters at Stoke Climsland, in the east of the county. Training for the men took place at Porthpean in St. Austell Bay, under the command of Captain Robin Williams, a tall, dark-haired, thin man full of life and enthusiasm as Susanne Carter remembers.

Her father, Walter Eva, was group leader of the four patrol units of Manaccan, Mullion, Porthleven and St. Keverne on the south side of the Helford. He was typical of the type of man chosen being a good shot and a farmer with a lifetime's knowledge of his home area of Manaccan. His sergeant was first of all Leslie Bawden, the local undertaker and carpenter, and after his promotion to 2nd Lieutenant, this position was taken by Harry Moore, proprietor of the garage at Zoar, north-west of Coverack.

The Manaccan Patrol was the first of the four to be formed. The six men who made up the patrol were two farmers, Wallace Rogers and Reg Lyne; two farm workers, Eric Bennetts and Vernon Ward; an oyster fisherman, Melville Peters, and a blacksmith, Harry Tresidder. Their underground hideout was in a corner of one of Walter Eva's fields, reached by a tunnel through a hedge.

Hubert Hicks in the old St Keverne hideout 1993 (B. Woods)

It was about the time of the fall of France that Captain Dingley began to call at Walter Eva's house and a priority telephone was installed there. He was provided with a uniform, a pistol with ammunition, a long knife and occasionally limpet mines, or as his daughter remembers them, "some horseshoe magnets with attachments." The patrols needed to find safe, dry storage for explosives, which in Cornwall's damp climate was not easy. The Iron Age fogou at Halligye near Trelowarren was used for a time, until the dynamite began to sweat.

The patrol was issued with iron rations and a keg of rum for "emergencies". It was useful to have a carpenter in the unit, because when this keg was later returned to the army, water had replaced the rum and sealing wax covered a hole carefully drilled through the cork!

If the Germans had landed in the South-West, all the regular troops in Cornwall and Devon would have retreated to a new defensive line stretching from Bridgwater to Axminster. The main job of the Auxiliary Patrols then would then have been to demolish the Royal Albert railway bridge over the River Tamar (there was no road bridge then) and set fire to the important oil storage tanks at Swanvale, near Falmouth. There was some concern about this second act because of the danger of burning petrol pouring down on the nearby houses. Luckily they never had to carry out either operation, but that threat near Falmouth was only too apparent one week before D-Day in 1944. (See "The Last Raid".)

Ray Lyne was a young boy when his father joined this organisation. Although he was secretive about it, equipment could not be easily hidden and Ray remembers the rifle with a long bayonet, which was later exchanged for a revolver and sharp knife. At weekends there were often courses for practising grenade throwing and planting explosives and his father "came home early one morning looking very pleased, having broken into an army camp on the St Keverne side of Zoar Garage and planted a dummy charge and detonator."

The men were kept alert and ready by regular training. The four patrol leaders met once a week at Porthleven and each patrol would carry out night-time exercises about twice a week. Perhaps it was after long hours in cold, wet winter weather that the emergency rum was appreciated! These men, like all other volunteers during the war, the fire watchers, ARP wardens, WVS workers, firemen and many others, still had their normal occupations to do during the day.

One of the later exercises by the Manaccan Patrol was to try and penetrate the defences of a radar station on Goonhilly Downs. If successful they were to leave a note on the guard house. Susanne Carter can remember the patrol gathering in the kitchen of her home with faces blackened and excitement mounting. They left their cars in an isolated part of the Downs, and stealthily approached the barbed wire boundary fence. They cut their way through and crawled silently towards the guard house. While lying in the ditch they heard the officer of the watch come out and speak to the sentries, who had nothing to report. They left their note and returned through the same hole in the fence and then back to the Eva household to phone the Commanding Officer. "He was shattered". Within a few days a crack RAF regiment with guard dogs was brought in, and

Auxiliary Units of Manaccan, Mullion, Porthleven & St Keverne 1944 (S. Carter)
Back Row: Hubert Hicks, Reg Lyne, Wallace Rogers, M. Plantain, Leslie Roberts, Gilbert Richards, Freddy Chegwidden, Eric Bennets, Melville Peters
Middle Row: ......, William Leggo, ..., Harry Tresidder, ..., Gerald Lee, ..., Sidney Williams
Front Row: John Gilbert, Frank Strike, 2nd Lt. Leslie Bawden, Capt. Dingley, Lt. Walter Eva, Sinclair James, Harry Moore

security was so much improved that when they did a repeat exercise they were caught at the perimeter fence by the animals.

Melville Peters the oyster fisherman, lost his home and scared the village at the same time. One night his house caught fire. He and his family managed to escape through a window in their nightclothes, but there were fears that the blaze could attract enemy planes. Firemen arrived but their hoses could not reach the water tank. The flames spread to his ammunition supply and helpers found themselves under fire from the exploding bullets. The following day, with his house in ashes, he had to sift through the wreckage for his officially-issued revolver.

After D-Day Captain Dingley was sent to France to assist with prisoners of war and for the last few months of their existence Captain Abbiss of Truro took over command for Cornwall. He had had his own patrol on the Roseland Peninsula with their hideout at Trenestrall Farm, near Ruan Lanihorne. Mrs Eva, whose husband farmed there, believed that the men who sometimes came into her kitchen to join her husband in his supper of bread and milk were part of the Home Guard. Their hideout was known about, but was strictly never visited. As she said, "You did not ask questions in those days."

Colonel Douglas, in his final letter to the patrols in November 1944, wrote:

"In the event of 'Action Stations' being ordered you knew well the kind of life you were in for. But that was in order, you were picked men, and others including myself knew that you would continue to fight whatever the conditions, with, or if necessary, without orders......In view of the fact that your lives depended on secrecy no public recognition will be possible."

What would have happened if the invasion had come? That is the unanswered question.

5. SECRET OPERATIONS

Secret operations have a particular fascination and Cornwall, far from the main centres of population and jutting out into the Channel towards France, is especially well placed for such hidden activities. The creeks of the Fal and Helford, with their tradition of smuggling runs on moonless nights across the water to Brittany, re-lived those days during the war. Innocent-looking fishing boats might be seen slipping out of these estuaries to rendezvous with French fishermen at sea or to creep silently into isolated Breton coves. Brandy and silks were not the object of these exercises; instead it was people and equipment.

Agents to work behind enemy lines with radios and other devices were brought to Cornwall, perhaps flying to Nancekuke, RAF Portreath, or to one of the other airfields, and then being hidden away from prying eyes until the time for sailing. Some left Cornwall never to return to Britain.

The Free French operated out of Mylor. In Book IV of *History Around the Fal*, reference is made to the small shed on the end of the jetty which became used "as a secret base for agents being shipped to France." French fishing vessels would appear and then disappear again. "French sailors were frequently put ashore and the Free French fighters supplied with their documents prior to being sailed across the Channel." Similar activities were organised from Falmouth by the SIS (Secret Intelligence Service) and in the Helford by the SOE (Special Operations Executive).

Both these groups helped prisoners-of-war and airmen who had been shot down to escape to Britain, but their main objects were different and unfortunately intense rivalry between them precluded a good working relationship in the early years of the war. The SIS landed agents to gather intelligence behind enemy lines and the SOE used agents for sabotage and for causing disruption in German-held territory.

Commander Frank Slocum, based in Falmouth for the SIS, wanted to keep the coasts of Brittany quiet, doing nothing to arouse suspicions and alert the lethal E-boat patrols. Commander Gerald Holdsworth, the SOE representative, was helping to carry out plans that could only rivet German attention on these same areas, as the Breton coastline was the most suitable for use by both of them, being extensive and less well-guarded than the shores further east. The two groups therefore worked separately and on less than amicable terms until 1943.

The SIS developed a regular route mostly using French fishing boats that had crossed over at the time of the fall of France, and with these they could

P.11 in Naval grey
& French colours
(R.Townsend)

come close to the Breton coast or perhaps rendezvous with the tunny fleet from Concarneau on the south coast of Brittany. Because the fishing boats were slow an advanced base was used in the Isles of Scilly. Moored between Tresco and Bryher, the boats were re-painted in French colours from their wartime British grey, but efforts had to be made to make the paint look old, as the French were short of materials for maintenance. It was discovered that throwing iron filings on to wet paint and then hosing it down with salt water achieved a suitably rusty appearance. With the men dressed in canvas trousers and smocks and the boats equipped with properly-marked flags and sails, they were then able to mingle with the French fishing fleet.

Richard Townsend became part of this Inshore Patrol Flotilla, as it was innocuously called, early in 1942 becoming first lieutenant to Daniel Lomenech, a Breton who had escaped from France and joined the Royal Navy. "We had a great respect for his seamanship and drive. The ship's company was devoted to him and would have done anything with him aboard." One of their successful operations was to rescue the wife and four children of their chief French agent, Rémy, as the Germans were beginning to close in on them. Rémy had organised a contact boat *Les Deux Anges*, a fishing boat from Pont Aven, to be the link between the SIS and the French

Rescuing Rémy's family. · Rémy and Daniel Lomenech nearest to camera
(R. Townsend)

shore, which for over a year smuggled agents, stores and letters into France. "The three members of the crew were absolutely magnificent", says Richard Townsend. "At enormous risk to themselves they made contact with us in all weathers."

On this particular trip they also brought back to Cornwall several large bundles of papers, including a plan for the coastal defences of France, smuggled out of the German headquarters by a painter and decorator, who concealed it in a roll of wallpaper before passing it on to Rémy.

Some months later they had Rémy on board again. He had flown back into France after the safe arrival of his family, but now needed to escape from the Gestapo. One new member of the crew for this operation was John Garnett, a young naval lieutenant who joined the group in November 1942. He tells of setting out from the Scillies, with radio sets packed in tobacco in sealed French petrol drums, and waiting for the rendezvous boat which failed to turn up on the first day. The following day she arrived and the radios were exchanged for Rémy and another agent. Richard Townsend remembers that Rémy was "particularly bothered by a very large parcel that he had brought out. This was eventually carried down to the wardroom, where with a fine flourish he undid the wrapping to reveal an azalea over two feet high covered in red flowers." This was a present for Madame de Gaulle who had earlier escaped to Britain, and for General de Gaulle he had a beautiful box containing soil from Lorraine, his home area.

This operation was completed without major problems, but it was not always so. John Garnett recalls some occasions when threat to safety came not only from the enemy, but also from the weather and at least once from his own side. They sometimes had to cross in gales of force 8 or 9 but as he says, "with those wonderful sea boats, if the crew could survive the boat certainly could." Fog was also a hazard as on the occasion when they were due to make landfall at the Penmarch light in the extreme south-west of Brittany. Visibility was so poor that they could scarcely see a quarter of a mile, but at last they heard the booming of the foghorn and then the breaking of waves on the rocks. As they turned away for safety they ran straight into an escorted German convoy. Behaving like an innocent fishing boat they sailed through, watched closely from the deck of the destroyer, until the fog swallowed them up.

On another occasion they were about thirty miles off the French coast, returning with agents from a successful pick-up, when they were suddenly bathed in the glare of a powerful searchlight. A Wellington bomber, searching for enemy submarines on the surface, had picked them up on its radar. Luckily, when they saw only a fishing boat, the pilot dropped no depth charges.

These fishing boats could take four or five days over one operation but later this In-Shore Patrol Flotilla gained a purpose-built boat to look like a Guilvinec trawler but with the addition of powerful engines. This could travel across from Frenchman's Creek on the Helford, where it was prepared for action, to the Concarneau fishing grounds off the Glenan Islands in one night and return within thirty-six hours.

In the summer of 1943 Commander Slocum moved from Falmouth and SIS and SOE activities were combined, based on the Helford, where SOE had been since late 1940. This group had been created in the dark days when Britain seemed to be alone after the fall of France. A Cabinet memorandum in July 1940 includes the following:

"The Prime Minister has further decided......that a new organisation shall be established forthwith to co-ordinate all action against the enemy overseas.........This organisation will be known as the Special Operations Executive." Churchill wanted to "set Europe ablaze."

Colin Gubbins, who was largely responsible for the Auxiliary Units, also played a major part in the setting up of this force. His aims were "to encourage and enable the people of occupied countries to harass the German war effort at every possible point by sabotage, subversion etc."

Commander Gerald Holdsworth was in charge of the Cornish section to begin with and made his base at Ridifarne on the north side of the Helford River near Port Navas, where there was direct access to the foreshore. This house belonged to the Bickford-Smiths and was willingly given up by them for the duration of the war. Appropriately the family were the makers of the safety fuse, originally invented by William Bickford in the nineteenth century, and now to be used by the SOE for their demolition work. As their operation expanded they took over another nearby house, Pedn-Billy, with its thatched boathouse.

One young sailor who found himself transferred to this Helford Flotilla in the summer of 1941 was Tom Long, a Norfolk man. He describes his first sight of the calm river shining in the summer sun, but as he was taken out to the Mutin, a French tunny fishing vessel moored there, he realised that this peacefulness was illusory; men (local shipwrights including Arthur Mitchell and Joe Paget) were busy digging out shrapnel from the decks, masts and boom and the sails were peppered with bullet holes from an air attack.

One of the men he found here was a French fisherman, Pierre, who had been hi-jacked off his boat in the Bay of Biscay by a British submarine, taken to London for questioning and then left in shabby lodgings where no one spoke French. He was rescued from this unhappy situation by Thomas

Cadett, later BBC correspondent in Paris, and became an important part of the Helford unit with his knowledge of the French coast and its fishing fleet.

Tom Long's first experience of a crossing to Brittany was in a seaplane tender RAF 360 when they dropped off two brothers, Joel and Yves Letac, and watched them disappearing into the darkness quietly paddling their canoes. Joel helped to organise one of the most successful SOE operations, code-named Josephine B, which was a raid on the Pessac electric power station at Merignac near Bordeaux. The demolition team, which had previously been dropped by air, later met up with Letac in Paris and they were forced to escape via Spain when they missed an aircraft rendezvous. They later heard that a dozen of the power station guards had been court-martialled and executed for negligence.

The seaplane tender was faster than the fishing boats, and had been provided by the RAF as a means of rescuing pilots who had been shot down. This journey to Brittany soon became routine. As darkness fell they would leave the Helford, quickly reaching the maximum speed of 22 knots and maintaining this speed until they were within four miles of the Breton coast. There they throttled back the engines for a quiet approach, and as

RAF 360, seaplane tender. Ridifarne in the background (M. Collins)

they crept close to the shore they would watch for a blue light giving the correct signal before they risked landing.

The system of landing agents by canoe had to be stopped after some of these boats had been discovered under a churchyard wall, which was being cleared of brambles just as Germans were passing by. In future all agents had to be taken ashore so no traces would be left behind. To overcome this problem Holdsworth's second-in command, Lieutenant Brooks Richards, designed and built at Portmellon near Mevagissey, "a marvellous operational scow made of plywood". This was flat-bottomed, easily man-handled and with detachable thwarts, which allowed them to be stacked on top of each other when deck space was limited.

Howard Rendle, a Port Navas man who was one of this team, has described an occasion when the boat landing them capsized in the strong surf and after righting it he then had to crawl along the beach, not knowing if it was mined, until he found cart tracks in the sand which he knew would be safe to follow.

The problem of landing the equipment that the agents needed, was dealt with in two ways. A "Helford container" was like a huge knapsack with a hinged lid and aluminium sides and bottom. It was carried by straps on

Attaching a canister to a buoy for passing on secret information
(R. Townsend)

the back so both hands could be free. Another method was by using underwater containers made of heavy metal about the size of a small dustbin. Plastic was not available in those days so waterproof silk was used for wrapping the contents. These containers were first tested in Falmouth Bay by filling them with sawdust, which was found to be still dry after three days. They would be left attached to a fisherman's buoy and the empties collected on a later occasion.

This worked until the Admiralty gave warning that French fishing vessels would be sunk, as the Germans used them as cover to plant mines and to shelter submarines. Commander Luard, liaison officer at St Eval who acted as guide from an Anson aircraft when they were trying to link up with the tunny fleet, persuaded the Admiralty to leaflet the fishermen before this happened to encourage them to come to Britain, and so avoided unnecessary bloodshed.

Tom Long describes the training that the team had to undergo. "Apart from silent rowing and canoe work we had to learn how to walk quietly on shingle beaches and how to find our way around using a map and compass." They were also taught different methods of combat both armed and unarmed. Bosahan woods, on the south side of the river, echoed with shots and the iron target figures lurking behind the trees "rang like a bell" when hit. They also did initial trials here for the "S" phones; the forerunners of walkie-talkies, later used by resistance groups in France. On the beach below they practised landing and re-embarking agents.

He describes one agent whom they were trying to train to get into and out of a scow. "It was really amazing how many ways he knew of capsizing". At last he seemed to have mastered it and when the weather was suitable the crossing to Brittany was made. On arrival he "was virtually lifted into the scow and held there until the stores had been loaded into a second boat." As the scows moved off, the agent, looking composed and carrying a box with a small white mouse given to him by the young sons of one of the SOE group, turned to wave good-bye, over-balanced and fell into the water. A dripping agent was handed over to the resistance.

Throughout the winter of 1941 the Helford Flotilla smuggled vital supplies into France and men both into and out of the country. On one occasion when they were expecting to pick up two agents, George Peake, a Newlyn man who was waiting on board, saw signals coming from all directions. "It suddenly resembled a boating lake as canoes and other boats crowded alongside" with about ten people, including two girls, eager for transport back to Cornwall. However the effectiveness of these Cornish operations was limited, partly because the seaplane tender was too vulnerable in bad weather and partly because of the opposition of the SIS.

Air drops were found to be more dependable and when sea crossings were necessary larger gun boats, based on Dartmouth, began to be used.

In the autumn of 1942, with the allied landings in North Africa, a new area of activity opened up and Gerald Holdsworth departed for Algeria with "his crew of unconventional sailors." One of the men who accompanied him was Deacon Rickard, a local man, who knew the Helford "as if it were his father's back yard" and was now to sail the coasts of North Africa, Italy, France and Yugoslavia, "carrying out dangerous and diverse missions, blowing up bridges, disrupting marshalling yards and now and then taking off one of our own agents."

Another man who joined them later, in June 1943, was Fred Sherrington, who had been on minesweepers before going to the Helford for about six months. While he was there he lived on board the *Roger Juliette*, another of the French fishing boats, with Pierre and George Peake and remembers times when they came back from having a drink at the Shipwright's Arms in Helford, put a trawl over the side of the boat and scooped up a bucketful of oysters, which were later devoured with great enjoyment. This hostelry, or occasionally the New Inn at Manaccan was used by the men, while the officers frequented the Ferry Boat Inn at Helford Passage.

Fred Sherrington's journey out to Algeria was done in style on a luxury liner where the passengers were expected to dress for dinner, but this was only a short interlude before the serious training for dangerous missions was continued. He trained with a small group of men, including Deacon Rickard and George Wilmot from Mawnan Smith, using small boats such as canoes and inflatable dinghies, ideal for ferrying ashore armaments and other equipment for their covert operations in Italy, where the allies made the first landings on the continent of Europe. Later, other men joined this group including Tom Long.

Those left behind on the Helford spent their time in training and testing, under the command of Lieutenant-Commander Bevil Warington Smyth, who had lost a foot while flying with the Fleet Air Arm. When the SIS moved their operation to the Helford in the summer of 1943 their new commander was Nigel Warington Smyth, his brother, whose base was the impressive three-masted yacht of Lord Runciman, *Sunbeam II*. This amalgamation proved successful and Bevil is reported to have said that it came as a source of surprise to more than one officer that the enemy was Hitler and not their opposite number in the sister organisation.

Tests on different types of surf boats were made at Praa Sands. The 14 foot SN.I, designed by Nigel Warington Smyth, was found to be successful and a 26 foot version, the SN.6, was developed. Tom Long recalls that these tests were only performed when there was a heavy swell crashing on

Sunbeam II anchored off Helford Point *(M. Collins)*

Testing a boat in the surf at Praa Sands *(N. Warington Smyth)*

the beach. They were done with minimum and maximum loads, while an Admiralty camera man recorded it all on film. This cold, wet work was relieved by frequent tots of rum and a visit to the Victory Inn at Perranuthnoe at lunch time for beer and pasties.

These tests bore fruit on the afternoon of Christmas Day 1943. Bad weather during the previous weeks had prevented the pick-up of a large group of airmen, and boat crews sent to do this had also been stranded. Over thirty people were desperately in need of rescue. On Christmas afternoon the seaplane tender towed the SN.6 down the river to meet a motor gunboat MGB 318 coming from Falmouth. The surf boat was then attached to the gunboat by a flexible grass rope and wire and towed across the Channel surfing on the stern wave of the boat, this delicate operation being carefully supervised by John Garnett.

SN6 in front of Pedn Billy boathouse.
Faces were blocked out for security reasons (N. Warington Smyth)

He recalls the amazing navigation of the gunboat crew as without lights they negotiated the channel into L'Aber Wrac'h, on the extreme west of Brittany, "which is hard enough to get into through the rocks in peacetime with lights." They threaded their way up the estuary on silenced engines and anchored. The surf boat, with Coxswain Howard Rendle and six other SOE men, then made two journeys to Ile Tariec, 800 yards away, to bring off thirty-two people. The return home was not without incident as the

SIS crew on church parade at Tresco. John Garnett on the right
(R. Townsend)

Howard Rendle, George Peake & Pierre in back row.
Capt. Wyndham front left (M. Collins)

Jimmy Holdsworth 28. 1. 67

Mary Holdsworth

Howard Rendle

George Duke

Bobby Harrington-Smyth

Frederick Brian Rickard

Tom Long

TREWINCE

Arthur Mitchell

Joe Paget

Frederick Sherrington

Joe Paget & Arthur Mitchell *(M. Collins)*

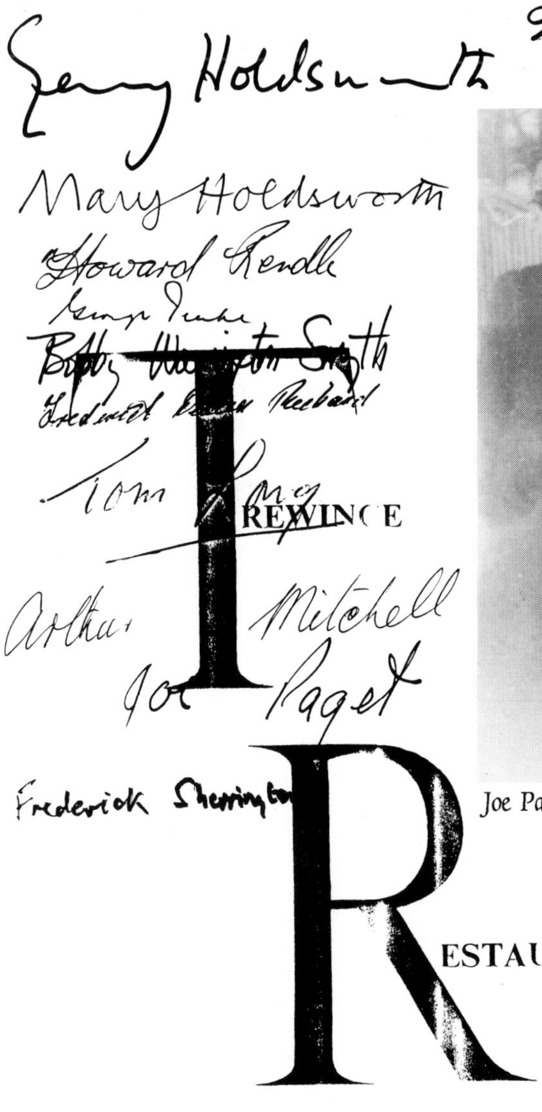

RESTAURANT

***PORT NAVAS**

SOE Reunion signatures *(M. Collins)*

engines broke down temporarily twenty miles off the French coast, but the coast of Cornwall soon made a welcome appearance.

One of the airmen rescued had parachuted out of his damaged Liberator believing that he was over Plymouth. He had stopped the first car to ask for a lift only to find that he was in France near Brest. Luckily for him the driver was an agent and took him to the pick-up point, so he was only one day late reporting back on duty. There was also a group of American airmen who had to travel from Paris by train to Brittany. As they spoke no French they were provided with false papers for the evacuation of a deaf and dumb unit. This worked successfully until a woman squeezed into the already crowded compartment with a pig which fell on to one of the men. His response was not that of a deaf mute. There was a terrible silence in the carriage but no-one gave them away.

Another of the rescued men was an agent, a professor of the Sorbonne University, carrying rolls of maps under his arm on which he had plotted all the flying bomb sites he had seen as he crossed France. This new weapon was to bring destruction, not only to London but to other areas in the south, before the sites could be finally destroyed.

This operation was the last to be carried out from the Helford, but as Sir Brooks Richards wrote for the Port Navas Regatta in 1993, "Howard Rendle's success in rescuing so large a group from a heavily fortified coast showed what could be done, and was followed by a series of some forty such missions from Dartmouth to beaches further east."

6. THE THREAT AT SEA

In October 1940 a mine field was laid off Falmouth. This was not to protect the coast from enemy invasion but was put down by German destroyers, now based in France, to threaten the vital shipping movements in the Channel approaches. The records show that the harbour was virtually closed for two weeks as a result from 5-17 October. Just over a year later the Harbour Master records, "Mines were reported to have been dropped by enemy planes during the night in different parts of the harbour and movements of shipping were considerably restricted." This was a constant problem during these years.

Winston Churchill later wrote "....dominating all our power to carry on the war or even keep ourselves alive, lay our mastery of the ocean routes and the free approach and entry to our ports." But this mastery was under intense pressure and came close to breaking point.

Falmouth has one of the best natural harbours in the world and was of great strategic importance, so the naval presence during the war was very noticeable. There were four naval nerve centres in the town. The Port Admiral, with other important officers, was based at Fort I in what is now the Membly Hall Hotel on the sea front. Here sixteen steps down under the lawn, camouflaged by "cabbages" made from a frame work of wire netting, there was an underground room for plotting the position of ships. The then Imperial Hotel, situated across the road from the Docks, became Fort II which dealt with mail to and from the ships and had the Naval Sick Bay. Fort III, the Pay Office, was situated above Taylor's Garage, where Trago Mills is today. When there was an air-raid alert in the early months, the Wrens working there would shelter downstairs in the garage with its petrol pumps, so the land mine that fell so close in March 1941 could have caused even greater devastation. Near the mouth of the Penryn River, at Coastlines Wharfs, was Fort IV, the base for the "little ships" of coastal defence.

Falmouth was not only important to the navy but also vital to merchant shipping coming into the harbour "for orders," or to unload desperately-needed supplies, or to make use of the important dock repair yards. When Hitler postponed his invasion plans, he hoped to achieve his objective by starving the country into surrender, so there was a constant threat at sea as well as from the air. German submarines, U-boats, lurked in the Atlantic and closer to the shore the menace came not only from the mines but also from the fast, manoeuvrable E-boats armed with torpedoes, which lay in wait for vulnerable shipping.

To counteract this threat, the Half-Moon Battery at Pendennis Castle, which had been dismantled in July 1938, was quickly re-armed and ready for action by November 1939 for coastal defence and to support the examination services controlling the movements of shipping in and out of the harbour. As the E-boat threat worsened construction work began at Middle Point Battery for a new gun emplacement, ready by the autumn of 1941 but not completed with searchlights until 1943. Similar defences were also built on the other side of the estuary at St. Mawes castle and St. Anthony Head.

The Half Moon Battery guns were fired on many occasions, sometimes at very long range, made possible by the use of radar information from stations such as at Jacka Point to the east and Goonhilly and Trelan on the Lizard to the south-west. An underground battery-plotting room was built near the Bay Hotel in Falmouth in 1942 where this information could be passed to the artillery men manning the guns.

In the cliff face at Toll Point, at the entrance to the Helford River, two French 75 mm guns were installed. They had a recoil of 48 inches which "was frightening to amateurs like us" recalls George Benney, one of the Home Guard who was trained to fire them. He describes the first practice session when they had to aim at a target being towed behind a boat. "We loaded and fired; the shell went over the top of the target. I brought the range down four hundred yards and was just short of the target. I pushed the range up a hundred yards and was right on target. Our regular army sergeant was a great big man and I was scared stiff of him. With my firing complete he pulled my sleeve and said, 'Bloody good shot,' so I was very pleased."

Many convoys of merchant ships under naval escort passed by these guns, sailing into the bay to and from the ports further east and north. The Falmouth Harbour Master's Records show days when there must have been intense activity with a number of vessels arriving or leaving together and other days when movement was almost non-existent.

These records, as well as the Police War Diaries, show that there were casualties apart from those already mentioned in the bombing raids. In May 1941 the *SS Octane* struck a mine as she was entering the harbour in a convoy. Tugs helped her to be beached off St. Mawes, but two of the crew died and two were seriously injured, the survivors being brought into Falmouth. Two months earlier "one dead body", three injured and twelve other survivors from the SS *Lemish* and SS *Nurgis* had also been brought ashore. Shortly after this a Polish ship was sunk by enemy planes off Coverack in Falmouth Bay, the two injured sailors being taken to Helston and the others brought to Falmouth. The *Mari-Flore*, sailing in a convoy along the north coast, was set alight by enemy action. Two burnt bodies were recovered, six were recorded as missing and the seven survivors were landed at Falmouth.

Ena Jose remembers "a ship in the docks called the *Coroni River*. It had been in for months being converted I believe into an armed merchantman. At last it was finished and went out into Falmouth Bay for trials where it struck a mine and sank; no loss of life luckily. There were crowds by Earle's Retreat watching it slowly sinking."

Air cover for these convoys was vital and in the early months of the war 217 Squadron, based at St Eval, provided this, but with the French Channel coast in German hands other units arrived to keep a watch for enemy submarines and surface vessels and as the war in the Atlantic continued to intensify so more planes came with the building of more airfields. In 1942-3 St Eval usually had four operational squadrons to combat U-Boats, although the rather slow and cumbersome planes were no match for German fighters, but as Eddie Walford writes in *War over the West*, "The St Eval airmen were undaunted by the task they faced. On countless occasions they limped back to base holed everywhere and with dead and dying aircrew who were prepared to give their all to keep vital sea lanes open."

In April 1942 Liberators were added to the strength of Predannack for long-range escort duty over the Atlantic, because the shipping losses were causing even greater concern, and it was from here that two months later a pilot gained a medal for his brave action in protecting a coastal convoy. Albert "Len" Harvey, already mentioned in the chapter on Air Defence, had a tobacconist shop in Falmouth and had joined the RAF early on in the war. In the summer of 1942 he was flying Beaufighters, patrolling the coast and escorting convoys sailing around Cornwall. One evening he and his radio operator, Bernard Wickstead, a journalist in peace time, were on a routine flight, when they saw a German bomber following the convoy flying so low over the water that spray was being whipped up by its slipstream. As he dived the German pilot spotted him and soon a fierce duel began, with both planes firing and manoeuvring for advantage. They were soon badly damaged, but neither gave up until the German plane lost an engine and finally plunged into the sea. The Beaufighter was too crippled to reach land and they ditched, cartwheeling into the waves about seven miles from shore.

Both Albert and Bernard managed to extricate themselves (they were the first ones to succeed in doing this from a Beaufighter), and with one inflatable dinghy between them, spent the next five hours or so alternately swimming and pulling until they were close under the rocky cliffs near

Portreath. Here they lost contact with each other as the dinghy capsized in the surf and they tried to avoid being dashed against the rocks. Albert climbed the cliff and found himself near to the operations room of RAF Portreath at Tehidy Barton, so he reported there and was later flown back to Predannack. He then cycled twenty miles home to Falmouth and was serving in his shop by the late afternoon. His comment in the Pilot's Log Book was, "Got a little wet." He was awarded the Distinguished Service Order and his operator the Distinguished Flying Cross.

The war on merchant shipping reached its peak in 1943, when over 100 ships were destroyed in March alone. In the following month the "Battle of Falmouth Bay" took place. It was on the night of 13-14 April when seven E-boats of the 5th Flotilla based in Cherbourg were lying hidden under the cliffs near the Manacles south of Falmouth. A convoy, number PW323, was unsuspectingly sailing past from Plymouth on its way up the west coast. The six coasters must have felt well-protected with two escort destroyers of the Hunt class, *Eskdale* and *Glaisdale*, and five naval trawlers. No doubt watch was being kept for any threat from the sea but the attack came suddenly from the landward side. The *Eskdale*, with its Norwegian crew, was stopped by a torpedo and then unable to manoeuvre was sunk by further hits. During the course of the fierce fighting one of the coasters, *Stanlake*, was also destroyed. This was happening close to the shore and the Reverend Nigel Eva, then a boy of twelve, remembers clearly the screaming of the shells and the shaking of the house as torpedoes exploded against the rocks. The *Falmouth Packet* of 16 April carried a report from German radio stating that two groups of E-boats had attacked that night, each damaging or sinking a Hunt class destroyer as well as sinking a merchant ship.

War memorials do not usually record the deaths of merchant seamen but their contribution was as vital and as dangerous as for many of the armed forces. One in four of all merchant seamen died, a higher percentage than for any of the armed forces, and yet without them Britain would have been starved of desperately needed supplies. The *Packet* reports in November 1943 of one Falmouth seaman who was luckier than some. This was Able Seaman Benjamin Cranwell, who at the age of 71 was repatriated from a German prison camp along with others who were elderly or wounded. His ship had been shelled and torpedoed by a German cruiser on 2 September 1940 off the coast of France when he had been wounded. He had spent the next five months in a French hospital in Nantes, before being moved, first to St. Nazaire and then to a prison camp in Germany. There he spent much of his time in the "excellent prison library". From there he saw, no doubt with mixed feelings, allied bombing raids "like firework displays." The food in the camp was poor and he

Robert Hichens (RCPS)

particularly praised the work of the British and Canadian Red Cross, whose food parcels had been greatly appreciated.

Fort IV, the headquarters for Coastal Defence, was crowded with the "little boats", the MLs (motor launches) MGBs (motor gun boats) and MTBs (motor torpedo boats), whose job it was to defend the shores and the shipping along the coast. From here the MTBs would set out in the evening for their night-time patrols on the look-out for their enemy counterparts, the E-boats. In addition these boats did escort duties and air-sea rescue work, the need for this increasing as the war dragged on. Trawlers were also used, often converted to minesweepers. They would join forces with three Norwegian whale catchers, *Kos* 14, 15, and 16 based here with their crews, for the unenviable task of trying to mop up the magnetic and acoustic mines before they could destroy lives and ships.

This is a reminder that defence of these shores was not just in the hands of the British Royal Navy; men of many different nationalities had found their way to this country and the Dutch, with their naval college at Enys House near Penryn, played an active part, not without tragedy. Their motor vessel, *Joma*, was struck by a mine in November 1941 when she was "on the St. Mawes Bank adjusting her compass." Three gunners were killed and the six injured were taken to the naval hospital in Falmouth.

Two local men who were honoured for their efforts in these "little ships" were Lieutenant Ian Trelawny from St. Martin near the Helford, a descendant of the famous sea-faring family, and Lieutenant-Commander Robert Hichens, a Falmouth man who had worked as a solicitor in Helston. Ian Trelawny was awarded the DSC for his persistent attack on an enemy convoy off the Dutch coast on 19 April 1943. He was in patrol with two other MTBs when they sighted a strongly-armed convoy speeding south. They quietly gave chase, hoping that the moon would stay hidden behind clouds. He gradually gained on them until, when only about eight hundred yards off, the moon came out, his boat was spotted, and all the ships began firing in his direction. He attacked and destroyed two merchant ships after a prolonged battle.

This success came just a week after the death of Robert Hichens. He had made a name for himself before the war as an international dinghy sailor and racing driver. He joined the RNVR (Royal Naval Volunteer Reserve), and took part in many operations in MTBs, mainly on the east and south coasts of England. The *Falmouth Packet* reporting his death on 16 April 1943, compared him to Drake: "he led his men into battle without weighing the odds, confident of their support in the tightest of corners." He had won the DSO twice, the DSC three times and had been mentioned in dispatches on three occasions. Ena Jose writes, "Great sadness was felt in Falmouth when a stray bullet killed Commander Hichens on an MTB

Barbara Kneebone *(B. Lorentzen)*

raid......He was a clever yachtsman and knew every inch of the coastline across the Channel and did untold damage there."

Robert Hichens had married Catherine Enys, related to the family who owned Enys House. In a history of the Royal Netherlands Naval College one chapter is devoted to their time at Enys House, and it refers to one particular episode when Hichens and the Dutch had worked together. Two Dutch cadets had been serving under him "during an engagement with some German E-boats not far from the Dutch coast" and set a booby trap or demolition charge over the side. The account goes on to say that for this action Hichens was awarded his second DSC, the first one being received for his activities during the Dunkirk evacuation. This incident is described by Hichens himself in his book, published posthumously, *We Fought Them in Gunboats*.

Today the Falmouth sea cadets training base is called after him and the Dutch also keep alive memories of these days by the name of *Enys* in their naval college.

A second Falmouth person to be honoured was Leading Wren Barbara Lorentzen (née Kneebone). The *Falmouth Packet* of 26 March 1943 records her bravery, when with a colleague she rescued sailors from a damaged ship during an enemy raid. "While the raid was still in progress they went at full-speed to the damaged vessel and were successful in rescuing several members of the crew". She remembers vividly today the enemy planes flying overhead, spraying the river with bullets while they dropped their bombs. The two Wrens picked up so many of the men hanging desperately on to the sinking ship, a collier the *SS Fernwood*, that water came up to the gunwales, threatening to sink the rescuers. On shore she helped to give first aid to survivors, some with nasty head wounds full of coal dust.

This had happened at Dartmouth in September 1942 and the young women had been recommended for the George Medal. When the ship owners realised some months later that they had received no official recognition, they scoured the country for a suitable present and arranged a special lunch at the Savoy Hotel in London. There Barbara and her companion were each presented with an inscribed, solid-silver powder compact. The *Packet* report of this occasion continues, "The captain and some of the officers were present and paid high praise to the bravery and resource of the young women under what were most dangerous conditions."

The losses in merchant shipping were dangerously high and were threatening to become even worse during these months. In March 1942 Falmouth was the starting point for a courageous exploit - Operation Chariot - aimed at reducing this threat.

7 THE RAID ON ST NAZAIRE OPERATION CHARIOT

One sunny March afternoon in 1942 a strange procession of boats could be seen sailing out into Falmouth Bay, an old warship escorted by a flotilla of little boats. Peter Gilson watched them leave, little knowing that he was seeing history in the making.

The news at that time was dismal; Rommel was driving back the Eighth Army in North Africa, Hong Kong had fallen to the Japanese and then Singapore had suddenly surrendered, a real blow to British prestige. Nearer home the menace on the sea was growing greater. German U-boat successes in the Atlantic were rising: before the end of February they had sunk more than half a million tons of shipping.

The great German battle cruisers were adding to the threat. The *Bismarck* had been sunk the previous year, but not before it had destroyed *HMS Hood* and nearly everyone on board. A careful eye was being kept on the *Scharnhorst*, *Gneisenau* and *Prince Eugen* in port at Brest, but they slipped out and sailed safely up the English Channel - another blow to British pride. Looming on the horizon was the potentially even greater threat of the *Tirpitz*, the largest and most powerful warship yet built. If she was let loose in the Atlantic the devastation could be immense.

She was so large that only one dock on the Atlantic seaboard could take her and that was the one at St Nazaire, built by the French before the war for their great passenger liner *Normandie*. If that dock could be destroyed the *Tirpitz* would never be used in the Atlantic. This was the background to the strange armada setting out from Falmouth on that March day.

The old warship was the *Campbeltown*, originally an American ship, but now converted in the docks at Devonport to look like a German destroyer. She was a moving bomb, packed with hidden explosives to be set on a time fuse. On board besides the small crew were carefully-trained commandos, and more were packed into the escort motor launches, each group primed to carry out a specific task. They had been preparing for some weeks, first in Scotland and then moving to Cardiff and Southampton to familiarise themselves with large docks.

Ena Jose writes, "No 5 Commando were stationed in Falmouth for training, their Headquarters being in Marlborough House. I had 3 billeted with me and what a task looking after them.....They trained along the coast and then left to do the raid on St Nazaire." Other accounts tell of them doing route marches up and down the Cornish hills and at least two were reported to have practised their marksmanship on turnips, which they sent rolling down a slope.

One Helford letter-writer was perhaps describing part of their training when she wrote on 23 January, "Apparently the commandos *invaded* the place about a fortnight ago and took everyone by surprise by invading from behind instead of landing on the Point where the Home Guard lay in wait for them." It was tactics like this that could ensure success for their covert operations.

The "little ships", some based in Falmouth, were more used to working in small groups, protecting merchant convoys and doing air-sea rescues, than manoeuvring in large formations so they had a short period of training, especially concentrating on approaching jetties at night time. As the boats and men began to gather in Falmouth secrecy became a problem. It was thought that there was a spy in the town so commandos and sailors were kept well apart at first, and a cover story of long-range anti-submarine sweeps was invented for the MLs with their increased weaponry and extra petrol tanks stowed on the decks.

The first time all the men worked together was on a two-day trip to the Isles of Scilly - no pleasure cruise this as the weather was vile and the commandos sea sick. Another combined exercise on the docks at Devonport was a dummy run. On this occasion it was found that the camouflage used was ineffective in bright searchlights and it had to be changed to a shade of mauve. It was only in the last days that the men were given any hint about the purpose of their training but not yet the destination. The plans were finalised, the men ready, their farewell letters written as advised, the tides were right, and with a suggestion of bad weather coming, they left a day early sailing out of Falmouth on 26 March, and only then was St Nazaire mentioned to the sailors.

They left their two escort destroyers off the French coast about forty miles from their destination. The small armada was led by a gunboat with the two commanders on board, Lieutenant-Colonel Newman of No 2 Commando and Commander Ryder. The captain of the gunboat was Lieutenant Curtis, who had taken a boat across to France on several secret missions when intelligence for this raid had been gained. Two MLs armed with torpedoes followed, with *Campbeltown* behind, and then six pairs of MLs filled with Commandos with two others bringing up the rear making up the battle order.

As the boats moved up the estuary of the Loire, British bombers were over St Nazaire to distract German attention from the river. Their orders were to attack the docks only if they could see them, but Winston Churchill had insisted that they should avoid the town to decrease the chance of

French casualties. Unfortunately the pilots had not been briefed on the underlying purpose of their role, so that when storm clouds obscured the docks, they circled for a time but then left much to the mystification of the Germans, who remained on full alert.

Sometime after midnight the moon shone mistily through the clouds on to the boats, now less than two miles from their destination, and then a searchlight picked out the flotilla. For a short time they were able to give the illusion that they were German, but when they failed to stop, the alarm was raised. They ran up the white ensign and "all hell broke loose," recalls Frank Axford, the radio operator on ML 270, one of the leading launches.

Campbeltown, under the command of Lieutenant-Commander Beattie, kept going at about twenty knots, broke through the boom defence and then crashed into the massive lock gates. ML 270 stood by, but about six minutes after the ramming it had a direct hit and lost the use of its steering. Nearby many of the MLs, vulnerable with their wooden hulls and petrol tanks, were soon a mass of flames, unable to unload the commandos, but some men were able to land from them and others swarmed over the sides of *Campbeltown*. In the chaos and darkness they were able to damage guns and demolish the pumping house and the two winding houses for the lock gates.

Bombardier "Johnny" Johnson, who now lives in Falmouth, was one of the commandos on *Campbeltown*. His specific task with four others was to blow up one of the winding houses for the dock gates. They climbed down the bamboo ladders hanging over the side of the ship, slipped off into the shadows avoiding German guards and found the building, but the doors were armour-plated and impossible to get through. They smashed the small window, squeezed through with their rucksacks bulging with demolition equipment, set the charges and then had two minutes to make their escape through the same narrow exit. Their operation was a success, but then they had to try and escape.

In scaling a fence "Johnny" Johnson was caught on the pointed top and lay there dangling, exposed to the firing until he managed to extricate himself and run to the dock side. There he saw burning boats and blazing oil on the water with men swimming and screaming. Their ML was intact but moving away. He made a desperate leap, grabbed the rails and was quickly hauled on board. But then the launch was hit and he found himself floundering in the water until he was washed ashore almost dead. His life was saved by a German doctor's injection and he became one of the many prisoners-of-war.

Only seven MLs escaped German attacks, some being destroyed by shore batteries on the return, and one took on a German destroyer for a while. Several joined up with their waiting escorts, including Frank

St Nazaire, taken from a British reconnaissance aircraft some time after the raid. Campbeltown in the dry dock (RCPS)

Axford's torpedo launch, which had escaped on its auxiliary steering. By now a speedy return to Cornwall was imperative as German planes were searching for them, so these MLs were scuttled and the crews transferred to the faster destroyer. Twenty two sorties were flown that day from St Eval and Predannack airfields to give cover for the vessels. Only three motor launches finally limped back on their own into Falmouth.

The *Campbeltown* blew up that day killing many German officers and sightseers. About one hundred and seventy British men died on the raid and many others were taken prisoner. Eighty-five medals were awarded for this one episode in the war including five VCs. One of these was for Able Seaman William Savage, who was killed manning the gun in the bows of the gunboat when it went to the help of some of the MLs fighting for their lives, and he was buried at Falmouth. Lieutenant-Commander Beattie of Mullion, who had kept the *Campbeltown* on course under heavy fire and steered her straight for the lock gates, was also awarded a VC. The *Tirpitz* never did venture out into the Atlantic as the docks were too badly damaged for use.

This amphibious operation, although costly in lives, had succeeded in its objects and had perhaps not only saved other lives in the future but had also pointed the way towards the biggest amphibious operation of them all, the D-Day invasion.

8. DIG FOR VICTORY

"No bananas, oranges, grapes or any imported fruit or vegetables, very few sweets; ration books for tea, sugar, butter, eggs; dried egg, very little meat and a lot of pleading for a bit of fat. I used to sit shaking the top of the milk in a jar to get about an ounce of butter." Ena Jose's memories are still clear on the problems of feeding a family in these days of desperate shortages, made even worse by the attacks on the merchant ships bringing their vital cargoes to the country.

In 1942 the basic weekly rations for one person were:

Meat	1 lb (offal, fish and poultry not rationed but limited)
Cheese	3 oz
Bacon & Ham	4 oz
Tea	2 oz
Sugar	8 oz
Preserves	4 oz of jam or marmalade or syrup
Butter	2 oz
Margarine	4 oz
Cooking Fat	2 oz
Eggs	1 fresh every other week (dried egg available)
Milk	2 pints

As the war dragged on food came under even stricter controls.

Clothing was rationed in 1941 after which it could only be bought with coupons, but even before then people were encouraged to be thrifty. Women's Institutes organised "make do and mend" sessions with exhibitions staged in Truro. At the Autumn Council meeting for the county in 1940, it was announced that 5,749 garments had been made by 1,582 members of working parties.

School children did their bit. The Mawnan Smith School Log records in November 1939: "Managers granted £3 for the purchase of wool. Children are making, chiefly in their own time, scarves, helmets, socks, mittens and pullovers. These will be sent to the men of this village serving with the Forces." In the following month the results were on display in an afternoon exhibition. "These articles have been knitted at home by the children (boys as well as girls) in Black Out hours." When rationing began the WVS organised clothing exchanges, where second-hand items could be swapped, which proved a very popular idea.

Dig for Victory

Fuel of all sorts was another commodity that needed to be strictly controlled. There were far fewer cars in those days, but private use was forbidden except for essential work. Many motorists took their cars off the road for the duration of the war. This could cause difficulty in transport, especially as bus services were also restricted. The Falmouth W.I Book mentions in 1941, "Members were unable to attend group meeting in Devoran for lack of transport." When the *Mari-Flore* was set on fire by enemy action in May 1941, the Police Diary carefully records, "possibility of saving cargo of coal."

Wood-pulp for paper-making had been imported before the war, so saving and re-cycling were the order of the day. Newspapers reduced the number of their pages; the *Falmouth Packet's* eight pages were soon cut to four, and the quality of the paper became much poorer. Big salvage campaigns were operated and local historians today can only bemoan the fact that interesting records were lost for ever, such as some of the Basset mining papers. The newspapers published results of the totals collected from the various villages and organisations, but the WVS Quarterly Report for July 1944 has an ominous ring. Under the heading, SALVAGE, it states, "In Cornwall the position is not satisfactory and a visit will shortly be made to the County."

The paper shortage was biting deep by 1944 when Mawnan Smith School Log records in March, "Sent amended requisition to District Clerk. It was very difficult to reduce the amount very much as the items had been cut to a minimum. Handwork and Needlework materials were cut but the Arithmetic and Geography Text Books are badly needed."

Metals of all sorts were also in short supply. Many people watched as the iron railings around their houses and gardens were cut down and carted away for the war effort. Aluminium was collected in huge quantities as an essential component for making fighter aircraft. The WVS (Women's Voluntary Service) nationwide gathered together over a thousand tons from such household items as saucepans, kettles and jelly moulds.

The fall of Malaya early in 1942 meant the loss of tin ore and wolfram. Cornwall has one of the longest records of tin production in the world, but by 1939 many of its mines had closed, the levels had been flooded and time and capital would be needed to open them up again, both of which were in short supply. However money was made available for some work and various mines and their dumps were prospected. Cligga Mine, on the cliffs near Perranporth, produced about three hundred tons of wolfram concentrates, and a few tons of alluvial tin were gained from the St Erth Valley, using the labour of thirty-two Italian prisoners of war, but generally speaking these and other efforts were uneconomic, although their supply was still important.

Dig for Victory

Bombing raids could damage water and gas mains, electricity cables and railway lines; equipment in the docks and on the farms might break down and need repair as well as machines in the quarries and mines. It was not only the raw materials that were needed but also the expertise, and with a shortage in man-power, women were recruited into engineering works like Visicks at Devoran, where they not only learnt to supply these necessities, but also helped to build Bailey bridges and gun parts for the military.

Armaments are costly so people were encouraged to give as much as possible to war funds. Each year there was a special campaign, such as "War Weapons Week" in 1941, "Wings For Victory Week" in 1943 and "Salute the Soldier Week" in 1944. Organisations raised money for their town or village's effort. Totals were announced in the newspapers and special parades, with marching groups and bands were organised. The *Falmouth Packet* reported in April 1943, "The Village Hall at Devoran was gaily decorated for the final of the 'Wings for Victory Week' on Saturday night. Mrs Dunn presented another of her delightful concerts to a packed audience". The songs included *The White Cliffs of Dover* and *There'll Always be an England'*, guaranteed to raise the rafters in those patriotic days. Clare Terrace School in Falmouth was given extra half-day holidays for its money-saving efforts on several occasions.

At Manaccan School the children had a 'War Savings Society.' "We take between two and three pounds a week," the headmistress said. "Last week it was nearly five pounds." The newspaper reporting this ends, "Manaccan, in fact, with five different savings groups, is saving and working for victory."

For many people the war was a time of thrift, conservation and collections. *The Story of the WVS*, published in 1959, states: "WVS was always collecting things, though it was not always absolutely certain why. Obediently it collected bottle tops and silver paper and bones and rose hips and sphagnum moss and tins. Rather more argumentatively it plucked sheep's wool off barbed wire and dug up acorns for pigs. Some members dared to ask why in thunder's name the pigs couldn't dig them up for themselves, but they were immediately hushed, handed a basket and directed to the nearest oak tree. Otherwise it was assured them, they would be sent to collect frogs." Perhaps this writer was dreaming of truffles when she said that acorns had to be dug up!

One very special commodity was collected on the rocks at Maenporth Beach in September 1943, when the tides were exceptionally low. This was the seaweed gonothyraea, from which the extract agar-agar is obtained, used in the culture of penicillin and originally imported from Japan. Bagfuls of it were collected for drying and no doubt many wounded people benefited from this antibiotic, which had only been discovered about fifteen

Time off for a Conqueror

Now Jerry is a "Conqueror"—and mostly very cross;
He arrests 'em and he shoots 'em
           just to show 'em who is boss.

But the British Tommy's different
        —he can't do what Jerry did,

Instead of shooting father he goes playing with the kid.

Now Jerry smashes everything—to show he doesn't care,
He steals their poor belongings
        —then warns them "If they dare . . ."

But the Men who beat the "Conqueror"
        (that's our Harry, Bert and Syd)

They'd rather try to talk to Ma
        —or mend things for the kid!

How can we show our gratitude to these men? The best, the most practical tribute we can offer them is to give them our complete support — by saving more. Let that be your salute to the soldier. **SAVE MORE.**

years earlier by Alexander Fleming. Once the Second Front was opened up the casualty rate would become even higher, so this was an important element of preparation.

Joan Belletti and Eddie Nabozna, a Sea Bee, gathering gonothyraea at Maenporth, September 1943 (J. Berntzen)

But it was food that was to cause perhaps the worst problems. Britain imported 60% of all its food supplies before the outbreak of war. The issue of ration books at regular intervals at least ensured that the dwindling stocks were shared out fairly with prices kept as low as possible, but for mothers with growing children it was a constant worry. Iris Dunstan can remember her mother walking the four miles or so from Penpol to Truro to queue up at the bakers for food to take away the pangs of hunger for her teenage family..

Queues were a normal sight outside shops. If you saw a queue you joined it. Perhaps some new delivery had just been made. One story that went the rounds in Falmouth was of a woman who joined a queue and when nearly at the top asked what it was for. "The Tales of Hoffman", she was told. "I'll get one and make soup," she was purported to have said.

The preservation of food became top priority to ensure that there was no wastage. Many houses had no fridges and freezers were practically unheard of. Even if they had been common, the disruption of electricity supplies caused by bombing would have reduced their usefulness. Food was dried, pickled, salted and bottled. Betty Phillips of Devoran remembers picking pramloads of blackberries and collecting and cleaning jars for the WI's Preservation Centre set up in the Village Hall, to make jam from the surplus fruit. The Falmouth branch recorded 630 lbs made in 1941 and 675 lbs in the following year.

Living by the sea meant that fish could be used to supplement the diet, but the *Falmouth Packet* reported in February 1943, "Shortages of fish supplies have resulted in considerable hardship being felt by those housewives who are sometimes at their wit's end as to how they shall provide the daily meal for their family."

People living by the Helford River had a windfall one day provided by the enemy. Bombs were dropped in the water and "everyone went out and picked up dead and stunned fish, so we had some free meals out of it," wrote one person. Perhaps this gave people ideas because one night, when a shoal of mackerel came into Carne Creek on a full tide, two members of the Auxiliary Units threw a stick of dynamite into the water from a boat and duly gathered up the stunned fish for distribution in the neighbourhood.

Harry Pallett recalls an unexpected bonus when he was working on Tregew Farm near Playing Place, not far from Truro. "A screeching caused me to climb the hedge and on the other side was a stoat circling round a petrified rabbit. When I jumped down the stoat ran off and I caught the rabbit which I duly handed over to the farmer." His unselfishness was rewarded because on the following day when he was returning home for his midday meal exactly the same thing happened at the same spot and this time it was his family who had the welcome addition to their meat ration.

Bartering was one way to bring some variety to the war time diet. Corporal Tomblin, who was based for a time at a decoy site near the Helford, recalls going with a local farmer to the Shipwright's Arms where meat was exchanged for crabs. "We came back with a boot full of very large crabs pulled in by local fishermen. The whole lot were chucked in the coal shed, where apparently they were able to live quite happily on coal until they were wanted for the pot."

In Helford village an elderly couple, Mr and Mrs Lugg, were surprised to see a rather large, round object which appeared on their garden path one moonlit night. There had been plenty of enemy activity in the area so they were, not surprisingly, worried and wondered what they should do about it. Mrs Lugg eventually urged her husband to get a stick and "poke en". The feared bomb turned out to be a large cabbage placed there for them by a kindly neighbour.

Vegetables grow early in Cornwall and were a very important part of the meagre war-time diet. "DIG FOR VICTORY" became a slogan as people

Dig for Victory

were urged to get rid of their flowers and to grow food. School children were encouraged to join the campaign. The boys of Manaccan School grew fruits and many kinds of vegetables including potatoes, broad beans and early peas in their quarter-acre garden. They sold their produce to their parents and the girls sometimes bottled the fruit or made jam.

The commercial market gardeners and flower growers were allowed only a restricted quota of flowers and in 1943, when the destruction on the sea reached its peak, a complete ban was put on flower growing so that all available land was given over to vegetable production. At least one local grower circumvented this ban and continued to grow some of the sweet-smelling violets for which the West Country was famous. Just before Christmas he travelled to Birmingham by train with carefully-packed bunches hidden in suitcases and found a ready market for his wares. The ban was lifted very soon afterwards because flowers were recognised as a morale-booster in the dark, bomb-damaged towns. Had these violets been appreciated by someone in authority that Christmas?

In the first years of the war the pony and wagon of Ron Hitchens and his father could be seen trotting along the almost empty road to Truro from their market garden above Penpol Creek, loaded with vegetables and fruit for the shops in the city. But 1943 brought a big increase in traffic as military lorries and jeeps raced along the narrow country roads; the

Richard Hitchens holding cabbage, his son Ron far right, with Italian prisoners of war and Dolly Rosevear, a land army girl (I. Dunstan)

American forces had arrived. The pony-wagon became too vulnerable so they acquired a car and trailer, and with the quota of petrol allowed them as food producers, continued to supply the townspeople.

Farming was a vital part of the war economy and land which had not been tilled for many years was brought back into production. The importance of this was recognised in the Police War Diary where on several occasions, when bombs had landed in fields, comments were included about the damage, if any, to corn crops.

However there could be occasions when military necessity overrode all else. Farmers at Nancekuke, on the north coast near Porthtowan, watched in dismay as their fields of corn almost ready for harvesting were brutally destroyed, as hedges were levelled for the building of the airfield. They never did get their land returned to them after the war as promised.

Manpower was a problem on the farms as in other areas of the economy with so many men in the armed forces. Those concerned with food production were exempted from the armed services but the work was labour-intensive. Prisoners-of -war were used; the Hitchens market garden had the services of two Italian prisoners, brought every day from their camp. "Very nice men," as Ron Hitchens recalls, who would make salads for themselves from the fresh vegetables they helped to grow. The most famous group of extra helpers on the land however were the land army girls.

Young women could choose to do farm work instead of joining the armed forces, and many "townies" found a completely new way of life in the countryside. Bosahan, the home of Lord and Lady Seaton on the banks of the Helford, became a training centre for the Women's Land Army (WLA). A newspaper report in February 1941 states:

> The last group - Misses Jerram, Hart, Purchas, Phillips and Annear - were tested at the end of their training by Mr Walter Tregarthen. They showed their skill in yard work, field work, chain harrowing, harnessing horses, carting turnips, cleaning houses, feeding pigs and milking. At the conclusion of the training all volunteers were dispatched to jobs that were waiting for them. "We have already a list of farmers that have booked land girls from the next batch....The principal demand is for milkers and girls for general and yard work. Some want girls to drive a car and take charge of a milk round. There is little request for tractor drivers."

One land army girl who not only did a milk round but also became a regular tractor driver was Gina Harrap. She came from London, with no

War Weapons Week Parade, Truro 1941

experience of farm work but with a great love of animals. Training lasted for just three weeks at Walter Tregarthen's farm at St Erth, where they were given the "short sharp shock treatment" of no breakfast on the first day, till they had collected the twenty or so cows from the field, "leaving the bull behind," and then milked them all by hand.

After successfully completing this training, including dung spreading and shock building, she went to a small fifty acre farm at Perranwell near Truro, where her duties included milking the small herd of cows and then going out delivering it in a Morris 8 van, which was always breaking down. It was not a case of just leaving bottles on doorsteps, as she had to fill each customer's jug separately, using her measuring dippers. She was a welcome visitor and was expected to be the purveyor of news as well as of milk, which was difficult as her farm employers had no radio or newspapers. The meagre butter ration was included on Fridays, and Saturday was the day for collecting up an assortment of bowls for the small amounts of cream that could be the special Sunday treat.

She then moved to the much larger farm of Mr Harvey Laity at Trefusis and it was here that she gained her tractor experience, ploughing the fields "where everywhere there was a view of the sea. It was beautiful." Here she had not only milkers but also beef cattle, pigs, horses and sheep to care for. She helped with the lambing, and on one occasion she rescued a tiny, muddy creature abandoned by its mother, to be greeted in later months by this now-boisterous lamb jumping up into her arms when it saw her in the field.

Her very first tractor-driving experience had been a nerve-racking one while she was still at Perranwell. She and a few other land girls were to take part in the War Weapons Week Parade in Truro in the spring of 1941, riding on the trailer of a tractor, but the tractor had no driver, so as she had some experience with cars she was put behind the wheel. All went well until the ambulance in front of them suddenly stopped. She desperately looked for the brakes, and came to a juddering stop just in time to avoid a collision, but throwing her colleagues into an undignified heap.

However much the men might have laughed in the pub of an evening at these girls' early attempts at a new occupation in a completely new environment, many of them proved their adaptability, stamina and expertise, to gain respect for doing a vitally important job.

The war had to be won by the military forces, but without civilian support in all these varied aspects they could never have succeeded. "Dig for Victory", could be the slogan not only for gardeners and farmers but also for all those people who dug deep into their pockets, their cupboards and lofts for salvage, and especially into their time.

Any dawn now this man may face his supreme test— the liberation of the enslaved peoples of Europe. Then, the ships and trains and trucks which normally distribute our coal will be used to rush supplies to the fighting men. That's why we must cut our use of coal, gas and electricity *now*, for existing stocks of coal are precious —*they may have to last a long time*. Fit fire bricks wherever possible, lag hot water tanks and pipes, go easy with hot water — small things compared with the job of our fighting men but essential if we are to give them all the backing they must have.

We must
SAVE FUEL
for Battle!

Issued by the Ministry of Fuel and Power

Music score cover for a popular US song in 1943

II THE FRIENDLY INVASION

9. "ALMOST THE 49th STATE OF THE UNION"

Early on Sunday 7 December 1941 Japanese planes attacked the American
naval base of Pearl Harbor in the Hawaiian Islands. In less than two hours
they had destroyed or damaged nineteen ships and over one hundred and
fifty planes, and killed more than two thousand men. Whether the
Americans liked it or not they were in the war. Within a few weeks four
thousand men had crossed the Atlantic to Britain; sixteen months later over
one and a half million American troops were stationed in the country
preparing for the Allied invasion of the coast of Normandy. This was the
largest influx of foreigners in the country since the Norman Invasion of
1066.

Even before December 1941, some Americans had arrived secretly in
Northern Ireland to begin the planning of new air and naval bases, and
before that Congress had passed the Lend-Lease Act authorising the
building of ships, tanks and other war necessities, and then leasing them to
friendly powers without any arrangements made for repayment. As
President Roosevelt said, "The best immediate defence for the United States
is the success of Great Britain defending itself."

The 29th Infantry Division, the Blue and Grey, embarked from Camp
Gilmour, New Jersey, and arrived at Greenock, Scotland in October 1942,
to replace the 1st Division which was moving out to North Africa to fight in
the Desert Campaign. They had crossed the dangerous waters of the
Atlantic without a convoy on the fast passenger liners, *Queen Mary* and
Queen Elizabeth, zig-zagging at a speed of thirty knots to outdistance
prowling U-boats. But it was no luxury travel for the nineteen thousand
troops crammed on board: as the vessels heeled over with each change of
direction, dishes slid off tables and men fell out of bunks.

Wire Corporal Michael Crawford of the 110th Field Artillery had joined
the 29th Division in January 1941, and was on punishment duty in the
kitchens of the *Queen Elizabeth* for being late back to camp. In fact his
conditions were better than for many of his compatriots, as he lived with
the British crew, eating bacon and eggs instead of spam and powdered egg,
and did not have to take it in turns to sleep in a bunk.

"Almost the 49th State of the Union"

As they were approaching Greenock they saw ships making ready to sail for Algeria. Perhaps they also saw the Falmouth pleasure boats, *Princess Victoria* and *Queen of the Fal*, which had been taken over by the Ministry of War for tendering work. When they landed they were quickly hustled on to trains for the journey south to Salisbury Plain. After several months training there and in Dorset, they moved westwards into Devon and Cornwall, to assume responsibility for the defence of the south-west coasts, and to gain experience in amphibious exercises ready for the landings on the French beaches.

A WVS Report described the West Country as "almost the 49th State of the Union". Huge numbers of American soldiers, sailors and airmen, increasingly took over cliffs, beaches, moors, fields, woods, houses, villages and towns all over the area. Roy Eva, a Royal Naval Artificer based at Torpoint, saw the changes come over the countryside on his regular journeys from there to his home at Park Farm, overlooking the Truro River. "I often wonder what the farmers did, because the Americans took over all the fields on either side of the main road (from Torpoint to Liskeard), for encampments and the storage of vehicles of all kinds." This happened by other main roads leading towards the ports, such as from Helston to Penryn. These camps were carefully camouflaged so that they would not be easily visible from the air, in spite of often being on open land.

US Naval Base, Falmouth

(J. Berntzen)

The Headquarters of the 29th Division was situated in Tavistock, with the 116th Regimental Combat Team based in the Plumer Barracks near Plymouth. In Cornwall, the 115th Combat Team used the barracks of the DCLI (Duke of Cornwall's Light Infantry) when the local troops there moved to Dorchester, with battalions camped at Liskeard and Launceston. The 175th was based in the Camborne area, with its headquarters on the Pendarves Estate and its troops based all over the far west of the county. In addition engineers, artillery, medical and other specialised units had to be catered for. With American airmen on the airfields and with the Naval Advanced Amphibious Base at Falmouth, the WVS Report was scarcely exaggerating.

"Almost the 49th State of the Union"

How did these young men, far from home and facing a very uncertain future, react to the strange country and people that they found themselves among, and how did the local people react to them? "How green England is in May," wrote one airman flying into St. Mawgan Airfield for the first time "It was as if England put on a show to welcome us." "Cold", "damp" and "dreary" were other reactions, and with this in mind the December issue of the magazine *Stars and Stripes* informed its readers, "Soldiers in the European Theater of Operations are entitled to one more pair of woollen socks."

It was not only the climate that they reacted to; some of the men had come from places deep in the interior of the States and were unused to the vagaries of the tides. A newly-arrived soldier was brought to his camp by the Percuil River at St Mawes at high tide, but when he awoke the following morning there was nothing but shiny mudbanks. He was astounded that the preparations for the invasion across the Channel should involve such an engineering feat! On Christmas Day 1943 residents in the tiny village of Point were alerted by faint cries coming from Restronguet Creek, to find one despairing American sinking into the mud as he tried to wade to the shore. He had missed the boat back from Falmouth to his ship in King Harry Reach, 'borrowed' a small motor-boat, but in the dark took the wrong turning and ended up in the creek on an ebb tide. Perhaps for him it was the Christmas spirit rather than lack of knowledge of the tides that caused his miserable night marooned on the mud.

The accommodation they lived in could vary a great deal. Some found themselves living in large, country houses and enjoyed the experience, even spending time looking after the gardens. This was the case with medical units stationed at Tregye and Killiganoon near Carnon Downs, where many local people have happy memories of the polite, generous and likeable young men who were stationed there. Another large country house, Pencalenick, was the base for a photographic unit, but some of those who camped by the Helford in the woods near Trebah Beach lived in primitive conditions, and had go to the nearby farm to be able to wash their clothes.

Many Americans were used to living standards which we would accept as normal today, but fifty years ago were regarded as luxuries in Britain especially in the countryside. In the villages, wells were often used for drinking water, fridges were not common and central heating was almost unheard of. Lavatories could be honeysuckle-covered earth closets at the far end of the garden and bathrooms were often non-existent. An English woman who moved from the north of the country to Helford half way through the war wrote, "....no electricity; oil lamps and cooking range; no sanitation, but piped water on our side of the village." Facilities in town houses were usually better as well as in the houses of the more well-to-do, but even here hot water and heating were not always abundant. This quaintness or backwardness took many of these young soldiers by surprise.

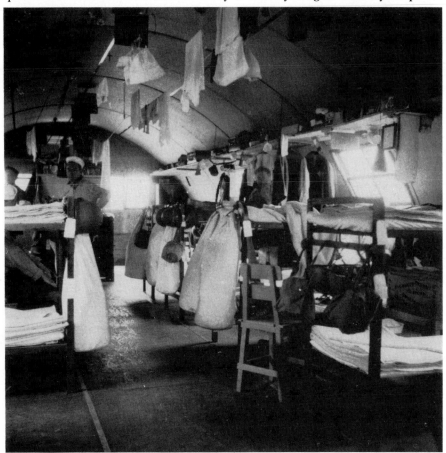

Men's quarters in US Naval Base (J. Berntzen)

When the Americans first arrived in the country, the war-time food seemed so bad that it threatened the morale of the forces and even their efficiency. They hated Brussels sprouts and the almost meatless war-time sausage. They missed fresh fruit, especially oranges, and fresh milk which was strictly rationed for the British, and also forbidden to the Americans because it was not all tuberculin-tested. So to keep up the spirits of the men, ships crossing from the States began to bring over not only weapons and ammunition needed for fighting but also food, even tinned fruit, which had disappeared from British shops soon after the war began.

"Almost the 49th State of the Union"

Market gardeners in Cornwall found themselves growing vegetables even more intensively to supply the demand from the Americans. Ron Hitchens started double or even triple cropping on his seven acres of ground at Penpol, growing not only the more usual vegetables of potatoes, cabbages, carrots and onions, but also sweet corn, a completely new experience. Every Monday and Thursday Mr Trelease, who supplied the American camps in the area, would place his order and on the collection days all would have to be ready by the time the lorry came at 8.30 in the morning. The working day could last for fourteen hours.

Training and duties would have taken up much of the Americans' time but they did have leisure to sample the delights of the area, where their friendly manner usually ensured a welcome. One young girl, who attended the Christmas social of the Devoran Women's Institute being held in the Village Hall, was watching the members sedately dancing, when the doorway was suddenly filled with smiling figures attracted by the sound of the small band. Within seconds, the ladies found themselves being whirled around the floor by their American partners in a most exciting way. Soon the visitors were teaching the local girls the extrovert skills of jitterbugging, much to their delight.

Pubs were also a popular innovation for them, even if they did not always appreciate the beer at first: Corporal Michael Crawford's first visit ended in his being violently sick. Bob Durbin, who was a lieutenant in the 776th Anti-Aircraft Weapons Battalion, which was based at Trelissick in 1944, writes "There we sang and played darts. I learned to like cider, even though they kidded me saying it was a lady's drink. I still like cider." Another way he relaxed with colleagues after a meal was to toss English coins to land on the front steps of Trelissick House. "The person who landed closest to the back of the top step got to keep the coins."

Many people opened their homes to the young men: Jean Nunn remembers them coming in on a Sunday evening and standing around the piano to sing Sankey hymns, and officers at Trelissick were "invited to a nearby manor to play tennis and have tea." Servicemen visiting English families could be very generous. Bob Durbin writes, "I would often bring coal or coke, extra food or candy. The families were very pleased to see us." One family, whose daughter became engaged to an American sailor based in Falmouth, was given food of all sorts and chicken cooked in butter, at a time when the butter ration for British people was 1 ounce a week.

Children also have happy memories of the cheerful generosity shown to them. Chewing gum, long candy bars, ice cream, ring dough-nuts covered in sugar, oranges, bananas; all these were new to many children and "Have you any gum, chum?" became a catch phrase. John Badger and his friends

American guns used to defend the Fal estuary

would wait for the weekly visit of the rations lorry to Durgan Cross, when they would be given "all sorts of stuff, sweets, chewing gum, cigarettes."

Soldiers often put on parties for local children, where the quantity and quality of the food as well as the fun and games, have been long remembered. Mick Edwards, then a boy of eight writes:

"The USA forces put on a Christmas party at Germoe School. All the local children went. My brother, Frank, and I had such a good time, candy, chewing gum, the like of which we had not seen. What a time! Magician, Punch and Judy, games, even a ride in trucks in a field behind the school. In the summer there had been a similar kind of 'open day' held at their camp on Praa Sands Green."

Clifford Penberth had his first taste of tomato juice from an anti-aircraft gun crew near Trelissick, "a real treat in 1944", and young Charlie Stevens, who lived at Tendera near the mouth of the Helford, was rewarded with chewing gum, sweets and occasionally large tins of pineapple and peaches, for keeping watch for a gun crew in the field near his home when they played cards. The day he gave warning of the approach of an officer he was given double rations.

Roy Eva, stationed at the naval base at Torpoint, would often hitch a lift on American lorries to gain a few hours at home near Truro. "I remember getting into the back of a lorry one day to find it loaded with crates of oranges. We hadn't seen an orange for years. One of the crates was broken open and we were instructed to throw out oranges to people as we passed through various villages. This was a lovely trip, it will always stay in my memory. The gasps of utter surprise and delight from people as an orange landed beside them."

Mick Edwards remembers an occasion when the rumbling of wheels announced the passing of a long convoy, always good to watch with its escort of military police, "snowdrops" as they were called because of their shiny white hats. He and his friend, Alan Jones, ran to wave to the men in the trucks and to their delight one man leant out and rolled two oranges to them across the road. "At first we thought they were orange-coloured balls. It was the first orange I can remember."

American vehicles were always a source of fascination. Jeeps with their amazing acceleration, quite unsuited to the narrow, Cornish lanes, carried stars and identity numbers, but many also had names. Mick Edward's sister would name-spot and record these in a little book; "Lucy", "Just Jane", ""Cannonball"", nicknames which were common in the USA. Bulldozers were another new experience for most children. Many roads needed to be widened, or have corners straightened to take the tanks and children watched this show of power with great interest, as happened at Mawnan Smith. The people who lost part of their gardens in the process might not have been so keen.

Not surprisingly accidents sometimes happened on the roads. Clifford Penberth remembers one that happened in the middle of Carnon Downs, when an army lorry crowded with troops collided with a local lorry. The army vehicle turned over several times and came to rest upside down. Some men were believed killed and the medical teams stationed at Tregye gained first hand experience in treating the wounded.

The stationing of so many Americans in such a comparatively small area could not be kept secret; they were swarming everywhere, but the local newspapers gave little clue of their presence. The occasional reference to "allied forces" was made, but rarely to "Americans". In June 1943 the *Falmouth Packet* reported on the "Wings for Victory" week in Penryn, where in the opening speech a welcome was extended to "several of our American cousins present", but no more than that.

The *West Briton* implied one of the difficulties of these days, with this short article:

When the Yanks say:	We say:
aisle (theatre)	gangway
vaudeville	variety
raincoat	mackintosh, mac
apartment house	block of flats
elevator	lift
shoulder (of road)	verge
automobile	motor car
battery (car)	accumulator
gear shift	gear lever
hood	bonnet
sedan	saloon car

The language difference could cause unexpected embarrassment such as the time when the landlady of a popular hostelry in Truro fell down rather heavily on her bottom one evening. The following day a concerned American officer called out in rather a loud voice, "Hi Mrs ----, how's your fanny today?" There was a stunned hush while the lady tried to hide her confusion.

10. "A DEEPER APPRECIATION OF OUR AMERICAN ALLIES"

What feelings motivated Truro people when there was a big National Savings Parade through the city in 1943? The American visitors led the march past the War Memorial, the Stars and Stripes waving and the band playing, to complete silence from the spectators. When the British servicemen appeared the cheers were thunderous.

The speaker at the Falmouth Rotary Club luncheon in January 1944 emphasised the need for a "clearer understanding and deeper appreciation of our American allies," and he made a reference to "harmful misconceptions". This shows that all was not sweetness and light between the British and Americans. The report of his speech added, "By the careful and interesting way in which he dealt with such a vital matter, as far as his fellow Rotarians were concerned, he succeeded admirably in achieving his aims." But of course there were many not present who were unable to benefit from his conciliatory words.

One of the problems was rivalry over girls between the British and American forces, with the visitors having the advantage. To many British girls these men had something of the glamour of Hollywood with their drawling speech, their smartly-tailored uniforms and their comparative wealth. A private soldier in the British army earned 14s a week, while his American counterpart earned £3 8s 9d, nearly five times as much. One Falmouth woman remembers that when the Americans came "the pubs and shops had a real harvest, they were all so well paid and had plenty of everything." In addition to the money, the uniform of the American private was better-cut and looked more like an officer's than the British private's. He also had a seemingly unlimited store of cigarettes and the sort of food that people in Britain had not tasted for a long time. British men might well be annoyed by this competition which was out of their league.

The Americans also provided entertainments that brought colour and gaiety to drab war-time living. Young women living in Falmouth were able to appreciate some of the top dance bands, such as Artie Shaw's, when they visited the town to entertain the troops. He ran the US Navy band which was stationed at Plymouth for some time. Whenever these bands played Glen Miller's "Stardust", the dancing would stop as the men and their partners clustered around the stage just to listen.

"A Deeper Appreciation of our American Allies"

British people also found themselves drawn into American racial problems. "I love the Americans but I don't like these whites they've brought with them." This is what one West Country farmer is reported to have said, indicating the general acceptance of black American troops by the British people. The idea of colour segregation was not really liked by many people, but this was the accepted system in the American forces. When they crossed the Atlantic they had separate accommodation on the *Queen Mary* and *Queen Elizabeth*, and wherever they were stationed the two colours had separate quarters. Near Durgan, white troops were camped in the woods beside the river, while the black troops used for road building, camp construction and maintenance, camped higher up the hill near Trebah Lodge.

Many British people had never seen black men before, but once they got used to them they were made welcome. Mick Edwards remembers the shock of seeing his first black person. He writes:

"One day, playing Red Indians, a group of us ventured into a small wood which we hadn't been in for some time. As we went in over the hedge we noticed some nets across the first section of trees. Not understanding what it was, we lifted it up to see why this 'curtain' ran across the path. As we did this, the first thing we saw was a big pair of shiny boots with white gaiters. On looking up I saw the first-ever coloured man in my life; his black face shone. We were too frightened to run, but we had no need to worry. He bent down and with a smile said that we couldn't come in......We left but not before we had each been given a little, flat box of 'chiclets' chewing gum. We treasured them and kept the packets long after we had eaten them."

At Devoran, coloured troops became a common sight, as they were camped nearby at Tullimaar House. Betty Phillips remembers one of these, who was welcomed by her parents into their home where he came to practise his violin. On his return home to the USA he became a member of a symphony orchestra.

There could be trouble between the white and black American troops, so segregation was often carried into their leisure time. Some places were open to only one of the colours, or if there was not much choice, then they were given separate times for their use. The Angel, at Helston, had 'black' and 'white' nights, and military police would regularly come round to the back door to check that everything was all right. However, in spite of these precautions, there were fights. On one occasion when Marjory Jones' mother served a black soldier before a white American in the Forces

Canteen, "there was ructions....a real racist fight and she had to call the police." David Brannlund remembers visiting the tented American hospital on the hill overlooking Truro, to visit the white G.I who was billeted in his home, who was recovering from a broken jaw after a fight with a black soldier. This occasion was made memorable for him by being given his first-ever orange.

There was a particularly unpleasant incident in Launceston when black soldiers, who had earlier been provoked, fired on two military policemen trying to persuade them to return to camp, wounding them in the legs. Joan Rendell was in the town that evening. In her book *Launceston: Some Pages in History*, she writes "....all hell broke loose in the direction of the Square. There was shouting and screaming; I clearly remember a woman's piercing scream and another high-pitched shriek which rose above the general din. Then I heard one shot fired. I cowered against the wall of the building, expecting to be engulfed in a running battle spilling down into Western Road. Then after only a few minutes but what seemed like an eternity, the 'snowdrops' (military policemen) came roaring along Western Road, jeep after jeep load of them, tyres screeching as they turned into the Square. More shouting, swearing, general hullaballoo.....I broke cover and scuttled back as fast as I could." The men were later court martialled and sentenced to death or life imprisonment.

Black soldiers were stationed at Perranarworthal, near Devoran and in *The Family at Rose Villa* Ivy Edwards wrote, "Dark American soldiers lived in tents in Edwards Brothers' Yard and officers were billeted at Goonvrea. On moonlight nights the men stole bicycles, later leaving them in the hedges. The soldiers received parcels of food from the United States and entertained local young women in their tents." It was this sexual aspect that white Americans particularly disliked and also changed some British people's attitude to the black soldiers.

Trouble occurred at Nanpean, near St. Austell, at a Wings for Victory dance, when a group of white soldiers came from the pub, pockets bulging with bottles, and a nasty fight with knives and broken glass developed between them and the black soldiers because they were dancing with the local girls. This fight lasted until the military police arrived to break it up. British girls often found that they were ostracised by the white GIs, once they knew that they had been out with black ones. Faced with this situation, many chose white partners, so further limiting the choice for the blacks.

Maurice Petherick, Member of Parliament for Penryn and Falmouth, seems to have been particularly anti-black. He wrote to Anthony Eden the Foreign Secretary, giving reasons why black troops should not be sent to Britain. He said that half-caste babies were bad for the country, that the blacks would have a bad impression of English women as only the lower sort would consort with them, and local people would be upset. He tried to get them sent back after they had arrived, and in another letter he wrote that a considerable number had been sent to his own constituency and added, "I hope it was not deliberate."

Although the British government did not officially support colour discrimination, after all coloured soldiers from the British Empire were fighting in the war, many were not happy with the situation. (Troops of the Royal Indian Army Service Corps were stationed at St Austell, who used mules for transport, stabled in the old cinema in the town.) Local newspapers came to report cases in such a way as to deter white girls from going out with black men, by always emphasising the colour if black soldiers were involved in an incident and implying irresponsibility by the girls.

In May 1944, the *Falmouth Packet* reported on two young girls from Penryn, "said to be in need of care and protection" and "out of control", who attended dances several times a week, stayed up late and "associated with coloured men." Both admitted misconduct and a coloured man, when interviewed, "admitted being guilty of certain conduct and had been dealt with by a court martial."

White GIs were not reported in the same way, although some women remember running the gauntlet of groping white hands which were far more persistent than any black ones. One Falmouth woman recalls being chased across the Moor, in the centre of the town, and up Jacob's Ladder when she had her two young children with her. In spite of the issue of condoms to the soldiers, both white and black babies resulted from these liaisons. On perhaps a happier note, some of the friendships made at this time led to marriages, and Cornish brides later made their way across the Atlantic following the route of so many emigrants of earlier years. Penryn Wesleyan Church was the setting for the marriage of Nellie Retchford to Philip Lee Bishop, of the United States Naval Reserve, whose home was far away in Seattle.

One other aspect that horrified many British people, who had suffered four years of increasing hardships, was the appalling extravagance of Americans, who often did not realise the privations that people were undergoing. Jack Paget remembers the lorries that would dump goods of all sorts in quarries at Longdowns, including clothes. "When you hadn't had a new shirt for some time, you went and looked in the dump." Clifford Penberth recalls the large amount of jetsam that came from American ships moored in King Harry Reach, timber and army ration biscuits, well wrapped and unharmed by the water, small packets of Nescafé, and even "a piano was alleged to have been salvaged" by a local person. Joe Gundry would go to the camp near Durgan in the evenings when they would be making toast for supper. "They would put a great blob of butter in the middle equivalent to a week's ration for us. I had never seen anything like it."

But in spite of all these problems the Americans were regarded as a 'good thing' by most people, lively, friendly, generous and easy to get on with. Certainly many innkeepers and shopkeepers had cause to be grateful for their free-spending ways. In Helford, when an army lorry got stuck in the narrow lane, the soldiers swarmed into the Post Office and for half-an-hour there was a hectic period of buying, while they bought up anything that was for sale.

*Wedding of Nellie Retchford and Philip Lee Bishop, US Navy,
Penryn Wesleyan Church (RCPS)*

11. PREPARATION OF THE CORNISH BEACHES

"For months we watched a change coming over the face of the Helford River. Where was once a green field a wide concrete road appeared leading to Trebah Beach, Polgwidden. .....Stretching out into the river from this was a pier of iron and timber construction. No longer had we an unbroken view of the peaceful river. Our quiet estuary was being mobilised for war - the Second Front." So wrote a member of the Mawnan Smith Women's Institute in later years.

The opening up of this Second Front had been long-discussed and long-delayed. The Americans on entering the war had agreed to give priority to Europe and North Africa rather than to the Pacific, the more obvious area from their point of view. But the full-frontal attack on German-occupied Europe which they wanted was felt to be inopportune at that early stage. However by 1943 the situation was changing rapidly. Already with the Battle of El Alamein and the Allied landings in Algeria late in 1942, control of North Africa seemed assured. On the Eastern Front, the German army failed to win Stalingrad and then surrendered in February 1943, after one of the most terrible battles in history. This was a turning-point in the war.

Another indication that the tide was turning in the Allies' favour came with an episode in which Cornwall played a part. The inventor, Barnes Wallis, carried out experiments with a football on Predannack Pool, which later resulted in his bouncing bomb that was to damage or destroy three dams holding back huge quantities of water in the industrial heartland of Germany. This Dambusters' Raid on 16 May 1943 was led by Wing Commander Guy Gibson, grandson of a sea captain from Porthleven where he had spent some of his childhood. He led the bombers in an attack on the Mohne Dam, where an exact height and speed had to be maintained and the bomb released precisely 400 yards from the target. After dropping his bomb, he kept flying low to draw fire away from the others lining up to come in. This was the first low-level night-time bombing raid ever to be carried out. They saw a tidal wave pour from the breached dam before they turned for the Eder Dam for a repeat performance. The devastation they caused was immense. About 1300 people were drowned, over half of whom were foreign slave workers unable to escape from their camp.

Factories, bridges and homes were destroyed, but it did not cause the industrial disruption hoped for. However the publicity given to it raised British morale and helped to encourage the Americans to concentrate on Europe rather than the Pacific. Guy Gibson was awarded the VC for this action, and by the time he was shot down and killed over Holland three and a half months after D-Day, he was the most decorated officer in the RAF.

Less than two months after this raid the first Allied landings in Europe were made on Sicily, later followed up by Italy. The time was ripe to complete the preparations for the main attack through France. Months if not years of planning were now to come to fruition. A huge army would soon be on the move and embarkation points had to be made ready. Three sites for loading heavy vehicles had already been selected in West Cornwall, one on the north side of the Helford at Polgwidden (Trebah Beach), and two on the Fal at Tolverne and Turnaware Point. These beaches had to be prepared, piers constructed and roads built.

Frank Curnow was appointed supervisor for the initial preparation for the beach at Turnaware Bar. He worked in the granite quarries at Porthoustock on the Lizard and was experienced in blasting, which was necessary on the rocky shore of the Bar. His work, with a small team, lasted from October 1943 until the following February, blasting, opening up a small quarry for hard core, laying and then levelling the beach with a steam roller (caught on one occasion in the rising tide), and making the surface ready for the concrete "matting" that would be placed on top. At the start of each week a lorry from Porthoustock Quarries came over the King Harry Ferry bringing dynamite, and collected the team on Friday evenings to take them back home for the week-end.

Accidents could happen unexpectedly, and one man suffered twice on the same occasion. One evening, when the warning for blasting was sounded, he was running for cover when he fell, hurting his ankle badly. The blasting was aborted while he was dealt with. The quickest way to get him to hospital was by boat, but as he was being transferred to the rescue launch strapped on to a stretcher, it slipped and he fell helplessly into the water. He was hurriedly fished out but no doubt one cold, wet figure must have arrived at the Royal Cornwall Infirmary that night.

The surfacing of the beach was carried out by the London firm of Harbour and General using flexible "matting" made up of sections of concrete pads reinforced with steel wire. This provided the hard surface necessary for heavy vehicles. Nowadays some of these mats can be seen paving local farmyards or forming garden walls, as at Tolverne. The same system was used at all three hards in the area and one girl living at Trebah

Preparation of the Cornish Beaches

Concrete matting still to be seen at Turnaware (D. Carter)

Farm recalls, "the beach and pier took a long time to build. I remember the turmoil it caused us on the farm."

The first batch of quarry dust intended for levelling Trebah Beach was brought there by the sailing barge, *Emma*. Labour was needed to deal with this and Frank Curnow, home in St Keverne for the week-end from his work at Turnaware, offered his services with some other local men. They were ferried across the river to unload about sixty tons by hand. They left it on the beach ready for use but an easterly wind blew up, the waves rose and much of this fine material was washed away.

Trebah Farm had its land split in two by the new road that had to be constructed down to the beach, which was started in early 1944 when black American soldiers arrived and set up camp near Trebah Lodge. Similar road access was needed to all the hards and this labour-intensive work was initially carried out by Irish navvies at Turnaware, building the long road there using sections made of concrete, a hardwearing material as can be testified today fifty years later. When the Americans arrived here, this road was considered too narrow and the black soldiers widened it by six foot "in no time at all."

This was not the only road widening that they had to do. Other roads leading to these areas needed altering. Even today engineers digging up the road from Lamanva to Mawnan Smith are only too aware of this when they strike the reinforced concrete used for strengthening the new sections. George Benney recalls that this was done in two stages. To begin with the verges were dug out and parking spaces made and concreted but later the road was widened throughout its entire length. In addition a large storage depot was established in the woods beside the road from Bosloe Cross to Glendurgan, where gaps in the hedge were made and the ground concreted to prevent its being churned up by the heavy vehicles using the entrances. The massive American earth-moving equipment and ready-mixed concrete, a new idea in Britain at that time, brought excitement to the village children and perhaps to adults as well.

Piers also needed to be built and John Badger remembers the tug *John Hamilton*, with its "Woodbine" funnel, towing a pile driver into the Helford. Sets of iron piles were driven in to form dolphins or jetties linked by gangways. The finishing touches of handrails, fenders and depth markers were done by the Penryn firm of Curtis & Co. Jack Paget, who worked at Turnaware, where two piers were built, recalls that the fenders were hefty six-inch-square pieces of elm eighteen feet long. They were hoisted up on to the stanchions to be bolted into place. He remembers one horrifying incident when a fender slipped, plunging heavily into the water. Luckily it surfaced beside his boat rather than under it as he feared and no more fenders were allowed to slip after this episode. Higher up the Fal a "T"-

Aerial view of pier at Trebah Beach, showing Dolphin tie-up facilities   (B. Woods)

shaped pier was built out into the deeper water at Tolverne reaching half way across the river.

Water was laid on to the sites at Turnaware and Trebah, quite a major operation in itself. At Trebah it was brought, partly above ground on posts, from Kergilliack near Falmouth, across fields and through Budock and Mawnan Smith to two large reservoirs installed near the lodge gate of Trebah House. At Turnaware a 6" water main was laid from a supply near the Pendower Hotel on the far side of the Roseland Peninsula, where it was pumped up over the hill and so down to the Fal. Jack Paget recalls being on station by the venting valve at the highest point when it was ready to start. He sat there all afternoon listening to the gurgle of water and thinking that it was never going to fill up, when whoosh, a jet of water shot forty feet into the air. He was soaked before he was able to close the vent. Pipes were extended on to the piers, so that vessels could easily fill their water tanks.

Pier at Trebah Beach *(S. King)*

Preparation of the Cornish Beaches

These sites needed protection: at Tolverne, for example, there was a gun site where the barbecue area is today and another one was set up on the opposite side of the river. Deception was also used as a form of defence. Decoy boats were built at Boscawen Park in Truro and Harry Pallett can remember "small, imitation landing craft" being built by a carpenter in Lamouth Creek, constructed of beer barrels held together by battens and then covered in hessian sacking. Mr Newman from Tolverne would tow these dummy boats around the river and anchor at different places to confuse any enemy intelligence.

Another form of deception was the use of decoy lights, similar to those used on Nare Head and Nare Point to draw attention away from Falmouth. To distract enemy planes away from Trebah, a decoy, or Starfish, site was built on the opposite side of the river along Frenchman's Creek, at Treveador and Trelean. Secrecy was so great that the electric cables were laid in sections, each one by a different group. At Treveador, one Nissen hut was used as the operating room and a second provided accommodation for those on duty. This was under the control of RAF personnel and Mr F. Tomblin, who was one of the operators, says that their arrival in the small village of St Martin aroused a lot of interest and curiosity and in spite of the land being taken over by the Air Ministry "a few managed to nose their way around." They never needed to activate their site "fortunately for the farm people living around."

Embarkation hards were also being prepared beside the Rivers Fowey and Tamar, but there was another type of beach preparation, a dangerous one, that was being undertaken at this time; this was clearing the sands of mines which had been laid down in the early months of the war against enemy invasion. Now these beaches were needed as training grounds and the Police War Diary indicates this change of policy. In the later months of 1943, before the clearing was begun, two incidents are recorded when American soldiers were killed or injured climbing over the protective barbed wire fences around these mine fields; one of these occasions, at Holywell Bay north of Perranporth, being to hunt for rabbits. But three months later there are reports of mines being cleared on both the north and the south coasts, with the Diaries recording fatalities that resulted at Perranporth and Treyarnon Bay on the north coast and at Par and Polridmouth, near Fowey, on the south. Soon beaches all round the coast were once again scenes of activity, not yet of holiday makers, but of the young American men practising their techniques for landing and trying out new, beach-landing craft.

12. TRAINING FOR INVASION

The South-West, especially Cornwall and Devon, became a huge training and preparation ground for invasion from the summer of 1943 to the fateful days of June 1944. The air, the seas and the land were full of movement and noise. Young airmen took off on massed bombing raids; children below would cheer them in the evening and count them back in the morning, watching many staggering low over the hedges desperately looking for airfields. Clifford Penberth, cycling from Feock to catch the school bus in Carnon Downs, saw American aircraft flying to British bases with engines out of action, bomb doors open and undercarriages dangling as they returned from night missions. Many did not make it either from these raids or from training flights. The Police War Diary records a growing number of crashed planes, many American, as the winter progressed.

> 23.10.43 American Liberator crashed St Mawes. Crew of 11 killed.
> 05.12.43 Crew of 10 American airmen rescued from sea approx. 5 miles SW of Isles of Scilly. Aircraft American Flying Fortress sank.
> 23.12.43 American Dakota crashed on summit of Brown Willy. 4 OCCS dead. From St Mawgan.

An earlier entry, for 12 October, records an incident presumably from a training flight. "A bullet from (believed) American aircraft penetrated roof of bungalow at Perranporth, came through kitchen ceiling and lodged on sideboard. Slight damage to bungalow, no casualties."

Five days after the Dakota crash on Brown Willy, another plane from St Mawgan crashed over the cliffs into the sea as it was taking off for a trans-Atlantic flight, killing thirteen of its crew and passengers. To add to the distress five men, who were attempting to rescue any survivors, were drowned when they were cut off by the rising tide. St Mawgan had been handed over to the American Air Force in June 1943 as it had one runway long enough to handle long-distance aircraft, and it became an important destination for ferrying in men and supplies from the United States as well as a staging post for planes flying to North Africa, the Middle East and India. As the build-up for D-Day increased in momentum it became one of the busiest stations in the country handling perhaps in one day over one hundred and fifty aircraft flying in from the States.

Training for Invasion

In the summer of 1943 fields on the outskirts of Falmouth suddenly blossomed with rows of Nissen huts as the United States Navy arrived to set up their Advanced Amphibious Base. Their camp stretched along Dracaena Avenue and up over the Beacon with its entrance at the end of Tregothnan Road. Sailors from this Construction Battalion (Sea Bees as they were called) would have the important task of helping to provide transport and support for the troops crossing to the Normandy beaches. The shortage in landing craft was a desperate problem and boatyards in Falmouth and further up the river were bustling with activity, especially in the weeks prior to D-Day, where the blindingly bright flares from welding torches was a sight remembered by at least one young child.

Jack Paget recalls "the biggest Nissen hut we had ever seen" built as a workshop at Grove Place in Falmouth. The Americans "put in a large concrete slab with bolts sticking upwards at crucial points. They then brought in woodworking machines of all descriptions, which slotted beautifully on to these bolts. The accuracy involved was incredible." He adds that they would drive the assault craft "like toys, flat out all the time." The steps at St Mawes had to be repaired several times because they hit them too hard.

Marjory Jones writes, "Everywhere activity increased, even on the remote beaches of St Mawes. No one knew why they (Americans) were there. Their main occupation seemed to be the creation of the most odd-looking boats. These looked like floating cattle trucks; the back and the front were capable of being let down to form ridged ramps so that it was possible to walk from the boat to the shore. They looked quite impractical and the professional old salts, who watched them working, did not know what to make of it. And not knowing what to make of it, they laughed and made the most of the contribution these youngsters from America had made to the village economy."

The roads now became much more busy and dangerous as the same "flat-out" driving technique was used with American jeeps and lorries. There was constant movement of troops as they were taken to infantry and artillery training grounds, sometimes miles away, for exercises of all descriptions.

Long route marches for basic fitness training had been endured on Salisbury Plain by soldiers of the 29th Division before they arrived in the West Country and for the infantry their journey west was one long route march. But so much more had to be done as none of these soldiers had any war experience; all depended on training.

The infantry, artillery and tank battalions needed plenty of space for their exercises and the moorland areas were the best available. Cornish engine houses, standing starkly on the treeless downs, were used as target

US Naval Nissen hut and crane
at Grove Place, Falmouth
(RCPS & J. Berntzen)

practice or worse for demolition practice, such as the engine house at Black Dog Shaft at Wheal Busy near Chacewater. Bodmin Moor provided a larger area for more extensive manoeuvres or long-range firing. Large guns were transported by night and hidden under camouflage nets during the day when not in use. At Berry Down, near St Neot, these huge weapons were fired across the moor to Brown Willy seven miles away. "The noise was incredible and our whole house used to shake" recalls Marshall Hellers, who then lived in a farmhouse nearby. But the most extensive training ground was Dartmoor in Devon.

"Dismal, very damp, foggy, windy and cold," is how Wire Corporal Michael Crawford remembers these wild, open moors, echoed even more graphically by Bob Hope's description when he came to entertain the troops: "Sewers with grass growing on them." His opinion of Cornish weather might also have not been favourable because his visit to the troops in Bodmin was in pouring rain and his stage was out of doors.

Michael Crawford's role was communications in the 110th Field Artillery, laying wire from the forward observer back to the battery. Much of his time was spent with the infantry doing rifle practice but he also fired the Howitzer 105mm guns with their 33lb shells with a range of seven and a half miles. "We had three types of shells, white phosphorous, regular high explosives and time-fused air-burst shells, which would rain down steel on enemy troops caught out in the open."

He was based at Bodmin in the DCLI (Duke of Cornwall's Light Infantry) barracks with the 115th Combat Team, but they travelled the forty miles or so to Okehampton so frequently that it was like a "commuter run." These troops were ready to be on the move at any time because their role was not only to train *for* invasion but also to defend the shores of Britain *from* invasion.

Crawling under barbed wire with full equipment, learning to handle explosives for blowing holes in barbed wire, using bayonets to probe for hidden mines, detecting and setting booby traps, learning first aid and gas drill, all this and more the young infantry soldiers had to become familiar with. Endurance and strength tests called "burp-up" exercises had to be passed to earn the Expert Infantryman's Badge and an extra five dollars a month pay.

The 175th Combat Troop had already shown their ability before they moved into West Cornwall. They had taken part in Exercise Columbus where they represented the defending "German" force against the British attackers, which included the 42nd Armoured Division. They managed to stop the spread of the attack, and a forty-mile flanking movement by the 29th Ranger Battalion destroyed the British headquarters and captured the attack plans.

The Rangers were like the British commandos and received much of their training in the even more Spartan conditions of the west of Scotland on the Argyll coast. While they were training there they took part in a raid on a radar station on a small island in the far west of Brittany - the Ile d'Ouessant. They travelled south to Cornwall leaving Falmouth in dories on the evening of 2 September 1943 , crossing the Channel without incident. They landed undetected, cut through the thick rolls of barbed wire, demolished one mast and part of the control station and returned without suffering any casualties. After the rigours of Scotland, the 29th Ranger Battalion was stationed in Bude on the north-east coast of Cornwall. There the work was more general with field training, lectures and forced marches.

Not all infantry training was done with large numbers of men. Ray Lyne, who lived at Kestle Farm near Manaccan, recalls seeing a platoon of about ten men spread out across a field. "I was there feeding the hens when a big Yank, a strapping great bloke, bundled straight over the hedge, landed amongst the chickens and a few strides later he was over the gate and down the field. He didn't deviate left or right."

Amphibious training was a vital ingredient for the infantrymen. For many of these soldiers the first time they had been in a boat was when they sailed the Atlantic for Britain. Now they would be expected to face a probably uncomfortable Channel crossing, transfer from the transporter ships to the smaller landing craft at sea, endure an even more uncomfortable time as the crowded boats made for shore and then land in surf carrying heavy equipment under enemy fire to win and then hold the beachhead. Mock-up landing craft were used for loading and unloading, nets were hung from high makeshift walls to practice climbing in full equipment, exiting procedures in columns of threes were practised and waterproofing methods for vehicles, guns and radios were learned.

Monica Cartwright, based at Fort I by Gyllyngvase Beach in Falmouth, watched constant activity on the sands below her as landing craft were being tested and men were gaining experience. One of the new amphibious vehicles being tried out here were DUKWS (ducks), designed to be driven straight from the boats, into the surf and on to the beaches. The main amphibious training grounds were again in Devon. The United States Assault Training Centre was situated at Saunton Sands on the north coast, where there are miles of sandy beach backed by dunes. At Slapton Sands on the south coast the most realistic exercises were staged and for this the local people were moved out of their homes so that this area could be turned into a "Normandy Beach."

Trial loading runs were made, as at Turnaware on the Fal, where practice proved that the time taken could be considerably reduced. In

Training exercise, Operation Duck, Christmas 1943 - GIs marching to Prince of Wales Pier, Falmouth (RCPS)

December 1943 a full scale loading and landing practice exercise took place, known as Operation Duck, with vessels sailing from the Falmouth area to Slapton Sands. A resident of Mawnan Smith related that it upset village life considerably. "Military Police called at each house stating that no cups of tea were to be handed out to any of the troops even if it was Christmas and they were standing around looking as if they needed cheering up." Because ships were in short supply only the 175th Combat Troops and the Divisional Headquarters were loaded after staying overnight in their "sausage", the name given to the marshalling areas from their long shape strung out by the port feeder roads.

Landing Craft at Falmouth, Operation Duck (RCPS)

Frank Axford, who was with a flotilla of motor launches used for air-sea rescue and convoy duty based in Falmouth during the winter of 1943-44, recalls one occasion when the launch he was on was used for General Bradley, the Senior Commander of the United States Ground Forces, to observe one of these exercises at Slapton from close quarters. He remembers most vividly the rocket launchers being fired from the ships, the noise, smoke and frantic activity giving a very realistic impression of what these soldiers might soon be facing. The time for training was about to end.

Operation Duck - Troops passing the Red Lion at Mawnan Smith (RCPS)

In the weeks immediately prior to D-Day, Slapton Sands became in turn each of the five Normandy invasion beaches, and to give realistic practice to all the naval and military forces concerned, live ammunition was used. The American forces for the Utah beach landing were mainly based in Devon, and disaster struck them on the night of April 27th-28th. The follow-up convoy consisting of eight LSTs (Landing Ship Tanks) all new ships, newly-arrived in Britain and with new crews, were suddenly attacked by E-boats based on Cherbourg. Two were sunk and one was badly damaged with terrible loss of life. It has been estimated that 946 sailors and soldiers were hurriedly buried and the whole incident was hushed up for many years.

It was to be hoped that these exercises would not only give the troops necessary combat training, but also highlight mistakes which could then be rectified in time for the real invasion of the Normandy Beaches. Responsibility for this was in the hands of commanders and Tolverne Cottage, nestling beside the water under the hanging woods of the Fal, must have been the scene for many important discussions, as this was the residence of some of the higher ranking officers. They took over nearly all the house for office and living accommodation, leaving just some of the back part for Mr and Mrs Newman to live in.

It is believed by many local people that General Eisenhower stayed at Tullimaar House at Perranarworthal, in the run-up to D-Day, visiting his officers at Tolverne. "He arrived by air landing in a field behind Church Town Farm and was taken down to the house from there", one person was told on good authority. Peter Newman's parents told him that they had been introduced to the General at Tolverne, and Jean Nunn believes that he came during a weekend when no Americans were allowed out. "There was a very uneasy feeling; something was happening but no one knew what." Perhaps this uneasy feeling was intensified by an uncorroborated incident that a shot was fired through the window of the house when he was there.

Lieutenant Durbin, the artillery supply officer based at Trelissick, when asked if he could confirm this visit writes, "There were all kinds of rumours going around the area but nothing was ever verified." Naturally no newspaper report was made on any possible visit - secrecy was paramount with the American presence in the area scarcely acknowledged.

Field Marshall Montgomery had an actor "look-alike" to confuse possible spies but almost certainly the visit made to Cornwall in March and reported in the local paper was made by the "real" man. The *West Briton* records him meeting pupils of his old school, King's School, Canterbury, which had been evacuated to Carlyon Bay. The more important purpose, visiting the American troops at Bodmin, was not mentioned. These troops would be under his command for the landings in Normandy.

Sh-sh-h-h!

The Germans are desperately anxious for any scrap of information about our invasion plans. An odd word, unwarily spoken, may give to listening ears the clue to a whole operation. Now, more than ever before, careless talk is dangerous. It may cost thousands of lives and delay victory for months.

What do I do . . . ?

I remember that what seems common knowledge to me may be valuable news to the enemy.

I never discuss troop movements or ship's sailings or convoys I have seen on the road.

I never talk about my war-work or the position of factories or deliveries of war material.

I keep a special guard on my tongue in public places — in parks, pubs, buses, restaurants, railway stations and trains, and when talking on the 'phone.

Whatever I see, learn, or happen to know — *I keep it to myself.*

Issued by the Ministry of Information

13. THE LAST RAID

A week before D-Day Falmouth suffered from its last and possibly worst air raid. The guarded *West Briton* report states, "This was the first time raiders had been over our shores to bomb during a moon period for about three months." It was particularly worrying as American troops with their vehicles were preparing to embark for the invasion of Normandy. Huge numbers were massed in and around the Falmouth area and vessels were crowded on the water, many hidden beside the wooded slopes of the rivers. Had the German Intelligence learned the details of the plan and was the invasion to be stopped before it was able to get under way? It was feared that there were spies in the area, so perhaps in spite of all the attempts to divert attention away from the South-West, the worst fears of the commanders were being realised.

About thirty enemy planes were detected approaching Falmouth soon after midnight on Tuesday 30 May. The leading planes dropped red and green flares to mark the bomb path and "window", strips of metallic foil, to confuse the radar operators. Then the bombers came in fast across Carrick Roads, the Docks, the Castle Promontory, along the sea front to Swanpool and on across the Helford dropping their loads.

The most worrying aspect of the raid was not mentioned in any newspaper at the time - censorship was much too tight. One of the huge petrol storage tanks, so carefully camouflaged in the hillside above Swanpool, received a direct hit, so destroying fuel vital for the invasion. The first public acknowledgement of it did not come for over three months, not until the invasion of Normandy had been successful and the Allies were advancing through France. On 4 September 1944, Herbert Morrison, the Home Secretary, in an Order of the Day, commended three local fire officers by name and the officers and men of National Fire Service Area 19 for their "admirable firemanship". The *Daily Express* then carried this headline:

FIREMEN FIGHT BLAZING RIVER MOVING ON VILLAGE
HOMES EVACUATED FOR TWO DAYS

"One of the most terrifying and spectacular fires since the days of the London blitz, was fought by men of the N.F.S. for 21 hours, it is disclosed this morning.

Gyllyngdune Firemen, Jerry Andrew and Cecil Miners, fighting the oil blaze at Swanvale (T. Eddy)

"The fire started when a hidden petrol dump in South-West England was set ablaze during an air raid.

"A great torrent of burning petrol rolled down a hillside towards a village, flowed into a river, and threatened to engulf the whole village."

Even three months later the newspaper account mentions no place names, but the village was Swanvale and the petrol dumps were those earmarked for demolition by the Auxiliary Units if the country had ever been invaded. Secrecy over this disaster had been strict. The account continues,

"When the bomb struck the dump a torrent of lighted petrol, flowing at about 1,000 feet a minute, came down the hillside and found its way into a waterway of a stream."

The population of Swanvale were being hurriedly evacuated as the flames from the ruptured petrol tank roared into the sky. Black smoke covered the area and burning oil was flowing down towards the houses.

"The N.F.S. men protected the village from the flames by throwing up a waterscreen between the fire and the houses.

"Not one house in the village caught fire although some were scorched by the heat.....The firemen then attacked the river of burning petrol with foam. One group fought upstream to prevent the fire from spreading, while another group concentrated on the burning petrol tank.

"Firefighters who directed their foam branches into the burning tank from further up the hillside did so with the knowledge that the ground on which they stood might collapse into the fire at any minute."

Foam was desperately needed and the naval stores, where supplies were kept, was locked and the key could not be found. A Wren, who had hurriedly gone on duty at Fort I received an urgent call and she gave the instruction, "Kick the door down."

In the early hours of the morning Chief Boatswain's Mate, Philip Lee Bishop, of the United States Navy was called from his home in Albany Road, where he lived with his wife Nellie (née Retchford) a Penryn girl. He became the hero of the hour by damming the stream of burning petrol and diverting it away from threatened houses. He received a British Empire Medal for "conspicuous bravery" and a Navy and Marine Corps Medal from the President of the United States "For heroic conduct while fighting a gasoline fire resulting from an enemy raid in Falmouth, Cornwall, England, May 30th 1944. Operating a bulldozer, BISHOP constructed an earthen dam which prevented the further spread of oil, and remained at his post until his work was completed, although the heat was so intense that he had to be sprayed constantly with water to prevent serious personal injury. His courage and fearless service were in keeping with the highest traditions of the United States Naval Service."

Philip Lee Bishop with bulldozer (RCPS)

But the fight went on for twenty one hours before the flames were finally dampened. As the newspaper report states,

"Petrol seeped through the surface of the hillside and formed pockets of oil. The heat caused those pockets to explode, sending up 'whirlpools' of flame, capped with black smoke, from 60 to 70 feet in the air.

"Three times the fire appeared to be out.....but the heat caused the petrol to vaporise. This created sufficient pressure to break through the blanket of foam, and each time there was a big 'flash-back', which set the whole area ablaze again."

To begin with the Gyllyngdune Auxiliary fire engine team spear-headed the fight against the flames, but gradually more and more engines arrived on the scene, some from miles away. One Auxiliary fireman, a master at Falmouth School, rushed all the way to Plymouth on his motor bike to fetch an engine, until as the newspaper account reports, "The fight involved twenty-eight pumps, two hundred firemen and five hundred American soldiers and sailors awaiting embarkation".

The Last Raid

To increase the pressure on the rescue services, the petrol dump was not the only casualty of this raid. Hotels along the sea front, many of them taken over by the forces for offices and accommodation, were also hit. The Pentargon and the Boscawen Hotels were destroyed and service personnel killed. The Police Diary records, "About 20 HEs were dropped in Falmouth Town in area of Docks and Sea Front.....2 residential hotels extensively damaged. 4 casualties in one, 2 naval officers, 1 security sergeant and 1 civilian. 18 seriously injured....A member of the US Service killed in the other hotel."

Bomb damage to Boscawen and Pentargon Hotels after the last raid
(J. Berntzen)

The Last Raid

The Wrens' quarters at Carthion and Cliff House were shattered by the blast, although luckily no one died. Not long before the raid some of the young women had been enjoying the Whit Monday dance at the Princess Pavilion. Now they had to face the stark realities of war. One Wren officer gained the British Empire Medal for risking her life driving lorries filled with petrol away from the flames.

Joyce Rees, the young manageress of the NAAFI at Pendennis Castle, was travelling back from Plymouth on the train when she heard the news that "half of Falmouth sea front had gone". Fearful for the safety of "her girls" she rushed to the Castle, which had been straddled by bombs, to find broken glass all over the room but the girls had taken shelter in time and were unharmed.

People living some miles away were only too aware that something awful had happened at Falmouth. At Devoran, some miles north of Falmouth, people could see in the morning great clouds of smoke billowing into the sky. They climbed the hill behind the church to try and see what had happened. It looked as if the whole town was on fire.

On the south side of Falmouth Bay at Nare Point, the "Q" site was activated for the last time by the two men on duty, one of whom was Richard Nicholls, and it brought down nine of the bombs intended for Falmouth, so saving the town from even greater devastation. Chief Petty Officer Moss, who was in command of the "Q" site, was off-duty at the Tregildry Guest House at Gillan, but rushed out with his dog, Lassie, clambered over a hedge and ran across the field to the control room, with shrapnel falling all round him. The area was soon covered in pieces, one measuring eighteen inches long and half an inch thick.

Mrs Lugg, who was at the guest house recalls, "I shall never forget the raid on Falmouth on Whit Monday 29-30 May, when the oil tanks at Swanvale were hit. We saw nothing but fire all along Falmouth beach. The whole sky was lit up.". The house was full with twenty eight guests that night who found shelter under the stairs, under hedges, or in the Morrison shelters in the garage.

The following day the site had to be prepared for action again, because it was feared that this might have been just the first of further planned raids. Edgar Chinn was picked up by the Curtis lorry to be taken there as usual, but they found the roads leading to Lamanva Cross choked with convoys of American lorries all moving slowly towards the embarkation hard at Trebah. Military Police were controlling movement and "jeeps were flying around everywhere".

When they eventually arrived at the site, the working party was not the usual naval one but American soldiers, with plenty of candy and cigarettes, Lucky Strike or Camel, so the workers did well that day. "It was a nice warm day, so we didn't have tea, but large tins of fruit juice, with fresh bread rolls, tinned meat and tinned fish. That really was luxury."

But the previous night's raid had been the Americans' first experience of enemy fire. They were "as scared as rabbits; any roar made them worried. The gunfire and the bombs of the previous night had really shaken them up. It was their battle initiation; they were really blooded that night." A week later the news was of the invasion of the Normandy beaches and the Falmouth raid must then have paled into insignificance for these men.

In spite of the momentous events on the far side, the fire fighters involved that night were not forgotten. The *Daily Express* article named the officers particularly commended by Herbert Morrison as "Fire Force Commander G Drury, Divisional Officer H D Cassini, Column Officer E Rayns as well as the officers and men of National Fire Service Area 19 for their "admirable firemanship."

III THE INVASION OF NORMANDY

14. EMBARKATION

"One weekend in June landing barges came up the river and lorries in a constant stream came down the cliff road to the beach and on to the landing stage. Through Mawnan Village the lorries came full of US servicemen all in silence. No communication was allowed between the civilians and men - no one cheered or waved. It was very solemn. From our house we watched the lorries packed on to the ships. We could see the men ranged along the side or moving about. For two days they remained. Then one morning in June 1944 they were there no more."

This sight, witnessed by a resident of Durgan, of the embarkation for Normandy at Trebah Beach, must have been repeated all around the south coast in those early June days. A large army was on the move needing support from huge numbers of vessels and planes. The logistical problems were immense and the preparations for embarkation had been building up for months.

From Bosloe Cross to the entrance of Glendurgan a large storage depot had been constructed in the early months of the year and there was a barbed wire barrier manned by military police where locals had to show their passes. "No relations were allowed to come and see us, just the village people only were allowed into Durgan" recalls John Badger as the security tightened in the area. Another person recalls, "On one occasion when going to Trebah Farm for the daily milk my daughter forgot her identity card and found herself escorted home by an MP."

These British Military Policemen, with their red caps and sashes, lodged in the stables at Trebah. They patrolled the cliffs in pairs and with their American counterparts kept guard on the camp. "We had warning shots fired on us at the time of loading," recalls John Badger, a boy at that time.

At Turnaware, on the east side of the Fal, a large number of Nissen huts were built in the trees, some being used for officers' quarters, and black ammunition huts made of curved iron were also scattered through the woods where their existence would not be obvious from the air.

American troops were pouring into the country, the monthly number peaking at 217,000 in April 1944. One of the units to arrive was the 776th

U.S. SECRET EQUALS BRITISH MOST SECRET

BIGOT

SUPREME HEADQUARTERS,
ALLIED EXPEDITIONARY FORCE

Copy No....

SHAEF (44) 22

10 March 1944

SUBJECT: Operation 'OVERLORD'

TO : Admiral Sir Bertram H. Ramsay, KCB, KBE, MVO,
Allied Naval Commander, Expeditionary Force,

General Sir Bernard L. Montgomery, KCB, DSO,
Commander-in-Chief, 21 Army Group,

Air Chief Marshall Sir Trafford L. Leigh-Mallory, KCB, DSO,
Air Commander-in-Chief, Allied Expeditionary Air Force.

PREVIOUS DIRECTIVES

1. COSSAC (43) 76 and COSSAC (44) 4 are cancelled and the following substituted therefor.

OBJECT

2. The object of Operation 'OVERLORD' is to secure a lodgement area on the Continent from which further offensive operations can be developed. The lodgement area must contain sufficient port facilities to maintain a force of some twenty-six to thirty divisions, and enable that force to be augmented by follow-up shipments from the UNITED STATES and elsewhere of additional divisions and supporting units at the rate of three to five divisions per month.

3. The operation will be carried out in two phases:-

Phase I – The effecting of an assault landing on the NORMANDY beaches between the limits of QUINEVILLE in the WEST and CABOURG-LES-BAINS in the EAST, to be followed by the early capture and development of airfield sites and the capture of the port of CHERBOURG.

Phase II – The enlargement of the area captured in Phase I so as to secure the whole of the CHERBOURG, LOIRE and BRITTANY group of ports.

TARGET DATE

4. The target date for this operation is 31st May, 1944.

Anti-Aircraft Artillery Automatic Weapons Battalion, which sailed from Boston on the last day of February on the *SS Boriquen*. After "what seemed an eternity" they arrived at Greenock in Scotland and were sent first to Monmouthshire and then to Cornwall, where they were based at Trelissick, overlooking the beautiful estuary of the River Fal.

There they were under the control of a British Royal Artillery Regiment, with their offices in the left wing of Trelissick House while the owners, the Copeland family, continued to live in the right wing. They set up 40mm gun positions here and elsewhere on either side of Falmouth Bay. The courtyard of the house was used as their supply base from where Lieutenant Robert (Bob) Durbin, the Supply Officer, would travel frequently to the different gun-locations. The King Harry Ferry soon became very familiar to him and he was known to the locals as the "whistling American," as he whiled away the time of the crossing.

Clifford Penberth, a schoolboy at the time, recalls the 40mm Bofors gun at Trevella and other gun sites at Pill Farm, Loe Beach and Turnaware. He also remembers the communications hut that stood on the quay at the ferry slip, where an Aldis signal lamp was operated by a man who was to him "a face at the window, cigarette dangling from the corner of his mouth" as he passed messages to the ships in the Reach. These ships were camouflaged with branches to merge into the woodland background and not be obvious from the air.

This build-up in the defences around the embarkation areas was an indication that the time was drawing near. From 1 April security became even tighter as "new protected areas" were declared making Cornwall effectively a no-go area for all without passes. The *Falmouth Packet* reported on a "young married woman" fined £5 for being in a prohibited area without permission, who had come to Falmouth "to see a sailor in the Allied Forces". This was just one indication of the control being kept on the movement of civilians.

Secrecy was of paramount importance and everyone was encouraged not to talk or ask questions in case vital information was inadvertently given away, for both the place and the time for this invasion had to be kept from the German Intelligence. The obvious place for invasion seemed to be the Calais area as it entailed the shortest crossing, but this was not chosen by the Allied Commanders because the Germans had defended the coasts here very strongly. However, ingenious devices were employed to give the appearance that this was the planned invasion area. Dummy boats were moored, dummy lorries parked and fake phone calls made to give the impression of heightened activity in the South-East closest to the Calais coast.

Embarkation

Although many people in Cornwall must have realised that the invasion of Europe was imminent because of increased activity, few people knew exactly when it was going to happen. In fact the invasion date had been put back on several occasions because vital parts were not ready. A TOP SECRET or BIGOT paper, as those concerned with D-Day were called, dated 10 March, mentions 31 May as the invasion date, but at the end of March it was realised that this was too soon and D-Day was deferred to June, although every effort was made to make the Germans think it was planned for July.

The shortage of landing craft was one problem and boatyards were busy desperately trying to fulfil this demand to add to the numbers that were coming in from the States. B.P.Allen, the Executive Officer aboard the LST (Landing Ship Tank) 508, remembers coming into Falmouth in March 1944 carrying a 125 ton LCT (Landing Craft Tank) on deck to unload at the mouth of the river. "It was quite a feat to launch it over the side of our ship" he recalls. LCTs were designed to carry up to nine tanks or twelve lorries, but it was the LSTs that were in particularly short supply. These shallow-draught vessels were designed with bows which opened up to allow tanks and trucks to be driven straight on to the shore down a ramp.

US landing craft at Grove Place, Falmouth (J. Berntzen)

It would in fact have been impossible to postpone the date beyond the first week in June when the tides were right - a low tide was needed as the obstacles planted by the Germans on the beaches were most effective at high tide - but the imaginative, floating jetty-complexes of the Mulberry Harbours were another problem. These were needed on the open beaches until ports had been captured and were in an operable condition. So many back-up supplies and reinforcements would be required after the initial invasion that unloading facilities were imperative and unfortunately the Mulberries had not been completed by the end of April.

The three main construction sites for these harbours were in the Thames Estuary, Pegwell Bay in Kent and Southampton, and an emergency force of welders had to be dragooned into these areas from other industries. When even this did not prove adequate Irish workers were brought in; not the best situation for secrecy. Other ports around the coasts contributed to the huge project, such as Falmouth Docks, and Charlestown Foundry near St Austell where iron couplings were made. It was touch and go whether the two harbours, one for the American beaches and one for the British, would be ready and without them the invasion would probably have to be called off. They were completed only just in time for 5 June, the new date for invasion, but there was no opportunity for practice with them. They were to be towed across the Channel on D-Day plus 1 to be assembled during the following two weeks.

As the momentum increased so did the movement in the air, on the sea and on the roads. Bombers from Predannack and St Mawgan flew out to attack railway junctions and bridges in occupied France, communication points being particularly targeted. Heavy raids were made not only on those closest to the Normandy Beaches, but also over much of the North-West of France so that German attention was not focused on the one area.

Ships began to gather in the embarkation areas and one small convoy of boats that passed the Cornish coast was a tug, escorted by motor launches, pulling part of the pipe line for PLUTO (Pipeline Under the Ocean). This was to be laid across the Channel once the invasion forces had gained a foothold on the other side and was the solution to the problem of supplying the huge number of vehicles, needed in the advance across France. Trials for this had been made across the Bristol Channel from Wales to North Devon near Ilfracombe, and by early 1943 petrol was being delivered to Devon and Cornwall at the rate of 38,000 gallons a day. This success led on to the more ambitious plan of the pipeline under the Channel.

Although the exact date was not known, many of the American soldiers guessed that it was to be sooner rather than later and that they would be leaving the places that had become "home" to them for the past months. A farewell party was held in Devoran Village Hall as a "thank you" for the hospitality the men had received in that area. Jean Nunn remembers the "wonderful food" and the room beautifully decorated with flowers from the gardens of Tregye and Killiganoon, where medical units had been stationed.

Boats loading for the D-Day assault in Falmouth Docks (RCPS)

By the third week of the month soldiers were being taken to their marshalling areas, the "sausages" by the port-feeder roads. Wire Corporal Michael Crawford, based with the 110th Field Artillery at Bodmin, remembers being told at 7pm on 15 May to pack everything including blankets and three hours later they were off, not to another hated exercise on Dartmoor as they feared, but to Antony House near Torpoint. Many of the 115th Combat Troops embarked in the Plymouth area, assigned to the second wave of troops due to land on Omaha Beach four hours after the initial assault.

The 116th Combat Troops, which had been in East Cornwall and South Devon, were attached to part of the battle-experienced First Division for the initial landings and they were transported to Dorset for embarkation from Dorset ports. The 175th, which was stationed in West Cornwall, was to land on D-Day plus 1 and many of these left from the embarkation points in the Fal and Helford areas. The roads were soon filled with men and vehicles rumbling by night through wakeful towns and villages.

After they had arrived in their marshalling areas security became tight, with the camps completely sealed off once the briefing started. Local people were discouraged from making any contact with the forces. Lilian Crocker, who was living in Tresawls Road on the outskirts of Truro opposite an American camp, recalls needing a pass just to go out and post a letter, and of being discreetly followed whenever she and her friend went for a walk, presumably to ensure that there were no friendly overtures. When her husband invited two Americans into his house to see his model railway, they were quickly rounded up and escorted back to camp.

The American Hospital on the hill above Truro was making its final preparations and other local hospitals were preparing to send patients home to make room for the military casualties expected. But in the camps morale needed to be kept high. Sergeant John Slaughter recalls that the officers became friendlier, they were allowed to sleep late, there were "tremendous movies every night", (Michael Crawford's group had Glen Miller's band) and they were fed with the best food they had ever had in the army, steak with all the trimmings and lemon meringue pie. "It was really fattening us up for the kill."

Until then the men had been given no details of place or time. Michael Crawford's unit started their briefing on 28 May. "We were shown scale models and aerial photographs of France and the places where we were going to go in." For most of the troops who had spent their last few months in Cornwall, this was to be on the beach code-named Omaha. Michael Crawford was told that the 110th Field Artillery was to go in with the 115th Combat Troops, following the 116th Infantry. "Once ashore we would pass through the 116th initial objectives near the beach and take an objective near Longueville and strike out for St Lo."

With so many men and vehicles to embark for both the initial assault and the follow-up, the loading operation needed to start early. Equipment and vehicles were loaded first and most of this had been completed by the end of May. Then it was the turn of the assault troops. For the 115th Infantry it began on 30 May at Torpoint, the day when Falmouth had suffered from its last raid. The 175th began loading on 1 June. "The build-up was over several days. It wasn't a five-minute flash in the pan."

Here and on the Roseland Peninsula the main roads were closed to civilians as military vehicles converged on the loading areas of the Helford and Fal. At Perranarworthal the road was choked for several days with slowly moving vehicles stopping and then moving forward again for a few yards. Bren gun carriers, which had been hidden there under cover in the buildings of Edwards Brothers' corn mill, now moved out to join the queue.

Embarkation

A resident of Mawnan Smith wrote, "For days and nights an endless stream of vehicles seemed to be rolling through on a much larger scale than ever before, for there were stores as well as everything else. Troops seemed everywhere. Village life almost came to a standstill. The last two days all traffic except the military was stopped. No buses were allowed and all the main roads were guarded, especially where side roads ran into them. Just one endless sound of wheels and motor engines last thing at night and still going on in the morning. A mighty army on the move."

Sylvia King recalls "When the vehicles moved along the roads to get down to Trebah Beach all civilians were suddenly ordered off them. We were at Mawnan Village School and forbidden to go home until our mothers had trekked across fields and hedges to collect us." Jack Paget, who lived in Mabe, saw the road filled with vehicles outside his house and out of curiosity went to see how far they stretched. He went as far as Edgcumbe, about three miles away and still the road was filled with jeeps and lorries, which tailed all the way back to Helston so he was told later.

Preparing for D-Day; US Naval truck at Grove Place (RCPS)

Jeeps and small trucks were parked under the trees beside the road from Mawnan Smith to Trebah, and the hard areas were filled with stores and larger vehicles all waiting to be loaded. Transporters slowly carried tanks followed by excited local boys. Men were busy sealing the engines with "handfuls of stuff like plasticene," so that they would be waterproof for the landing through the surf. Michael Crawford's group was doing the same thing with guns and radios as they waited at Antony House, where they were also supplied with French money. Beside the roads leading to Turnaware troops sat on the grass verges by their vehicles cooking food as they waited to move down to the embarkation hard. At Tolverne at least thirteen LSTs, which had been moored in the creek for some time, arrived in turn to load troops, guns and vehicles, before moving slowly off downstream passing the similarly busy scene at Turnaware.

One of the men who embarked here on 4 June was Philip C Bowers from the Headquarters of the V Corps G3 Section, who landed on Omaha Beach two days later and survived to record this in 1977 in the Visitors' Book.

Much of the loading was done at night as John Badger remembers, witnessing the sight on the Helford. "The LSTs were very large, two loading at a time, one on each side of the pier, and the vehicles drove

Loading for D-Day at Trebah Beach (RCPS)

140

down the road and straight on. A mass of very big stuff came through, large tanks, Bren gun carriers and track-driven trucks. Foot soldiers with the convoy were off-loaded on the beach and walked up the gangway on to the jetty and so on to the boat." Watchers at Golden Gear, opposite Trebah Beach, clearly heard across the water the men being counted on board. On one night the quickly-receding spring tide caught the boats on the mud and tugs had to be brought in to pull them into the deeper water. Dennis Cannicott remembers looking down the road to the beach in the night where they saw "tiny lights winding all the way down the cliff road. The river appeared to be full of LSTs."

At Fowey vessels were packed so tightly on the water that it would have been possible to walk dry shod from one side of the river to the other. The Fal was also filled with vessels and a ban was put on all the area around the river. Clifford Penberth remembers Carrick Roads and King Harry Reach, close to Turnaware and Tolverne, "packed with LSTs", and orders were heard being given through loudspeakers. In Falmouth itself tents sprang up in the area of the Docks by Grove Place and up Arwenack Avenue, the men camping there overnight. "The smell of their supper cooking was delicious," as Joan Berntzen recalls. One young woman, seeing the armoured vehicles travelling along Western Terrace with the soldiers laughing and singing, was crying when she arrived home wondering how many of those young men would be returning.

At Antony House the last preparations were being made and then the 110th Field Artillery were loaded aboard five British LCTs on the river at St Germans, which when filled moved out into Plymouth Harbour. Roy Eva watched preparations from HMS Fisgard on the hill above Torpoint. "The amount of traffic was incredible as was the noise. This went on for three or four days, with transporters, tanks, lorries, vehicles of all descriptions." The huge armada set sail on 4 June, only to be recalled, as the last postponement had been made, this time because of rough weather.

These were particularly worrying times for the high command because so much depended on a safe crossing of the Channel. The weather forecast for 5 June was for storms which could have brought disaster. Would this improve for the following day because if not the tides would make successful landings much more unlikely after this. One of the senior members of the team responsible for producing the weather forecast to be studied by the commanders was Professor Sverre Petterssen, a Norwegian meteorological expert, who had come to Britain from America in 1942 as a Lieutenant Colonel in the Norwegian Air Force. General Eisenhower later wrote to thank him for the "advice necessary for the selection of D-Day.......the information received was the best obtainable." This team

Troops waiting for D-Day embarkation at Falmouth *(RCPS)*

forecast a short improvement in the weather for the following day, so the decision was taken.

Supreme Headquarters
ALLIED EXPEDITIONARY FORCE
Office of the Supreme Commander

19 September 1944

Dear Dr. Pettersen,

I desire to commend you for your part in the coordination of the operation of the Meteorological Service in support of the 'OVERLORD' assault of the Continent of Europe. Considerable research and long hours of work by you and your associates resulted in the reconciliation of differences in forecasting methods and the development of a procedure which enabled me to receive the advice necessary for the selection of D-day with confidence that the information received was the best obtainable.

This service on your part, and those associated with you is sincerely appreciated and merits very special commendation as an outstanding contribution to the success of the Allied invasion.

Sincerely,
Dwight D. Eisenhower

Dr. Sverre Petterssen
Meteorological Office
Air Ministry
London, W.C.2.

Michael Crawford of the 110th Field Artillery found himself setting off once more twenty-four hours later, packed so tightly on board that "I thought that we were going to sink with the load. All you could see were balloons and three columns of landing craft protected by destroyers and cruisers on the outside." Some men were even being transported in open ocean-going rafts towed behind the landing craft.

On a warm day in early June people were picnicking on Porthallow Beach when "to our amazement we saw an armada of landing craft going out to sea." Sixth formers looking out of the window at school in Penzance saw Mounts Bay filled with ships. The LSTs (Landing Ships Tank) and LSIs (Landing Ships Infantry) were leaving the coasts of Cornwall behind. Operation Neptune was under way and the invasion of Normandy was about to begin. When the restrictions on civilians around the Fal and Helford were lifted the rivers and the harbour were empty. As Joe Gundry says, "One minute the whole place was packed, the next they had all gone." Another man recalls, "There was nothing but an eerie silence."

15. THE BBC

Most people first heard of the landings in Normandy from the BBC announcement on the morning of 6 June. The radio, or "wireless" as it was then called, provided a method of mass-communication unavailable in any previous war and so the BBC had a very important part to play. "My parents had acquired a wireless in 1937 after being connected to the electricity in Trevella, Feock," writes Clifford Penberth. "My father listened to the news when it was broadcast during the evening and woe betide any child who made any utterance during that time."

There were dangers inherent in passing on information in this way as the 1940 leaflet "Beating the Invader" makes clear. To the question "Will instructions be given over the wireless?" the answer was, "Yes; so far as possible. But remember that the enemy can overhear any wireless message, so that the wireless cannot be used for any instructions which might give him valuable information."

There was also another problem: enemy aircraft could home in on the radio transmitters, and the Luftwaffe had every pre-war transmitter pinpointed on their maps. To solve this, low-powered transmitters were mounted on lorries which would transmit broadcasts during air raid alerts when the fixed transmitters would be switched off or have their power reduced.

One hundred watt transmitters were installed all over the country and one of these was at Redruth, housed in two adjacent garages in a yard. One garage was for the transmitter and the other was used as the office for the operators. Conditions were primitive, with one small oil stove for heating and a lavatory and wash basin in a shed at the far side of the yard. The transmitter radiated only during the day but there was always a night shift to keep contact with Plymouth and the local military.

When an Air Raid Warning Red was given, they shut down the transmitter until the All Clear was sounded. Mary Baker, who was one of the small band of operators there remembers, "We had so many "Reds" that one girl in Plymouth wondered how we could stand such bombing, but in fact the alerts were given, not because we were a special target, but because the bombers were flying over to attack ships in the Bristol Channel when the convoys left them, and the transmitters were shut down to prevent them using the signal to determine their position."

The Germans could also make use of this easy way to enter people's homes. Programmes were interrupted by the voice of William Joyce, Lord Haw Haw as he was nicknamed, broadcasting German propaganda. During the early months of 1941 St Eval suffered from almost nightly air raids and on many occasions he referred to it as a main target for the bombers of the Luftwaffe He also mentioned bombing of the arsenic works at Bissoe, but these had long been closed. He was doing his best to depress British morale, but the BBC proved to be an important medium for raising people's spirits.

Winston Churchill's speeches, either reported from parliament or broadcast direct to the country, have been long-remembered for their graphic use of words which appealed to the feelings of the time. Comedy programmes, which could make people laugh during the dark days of destruction, were obvious morale boosters: Tommy Handley's *Itma* and *Bandwagon* with Arthur Askey and Richard Murdoch became compulsive listening for many.

In 1943, with American troops pouring into the county in ever increasing numbers, a new radio station was built at Lanner on the high ground above Redruth, with two 10 KW transmitters, one for Home Services and one for the Forces Network. There was some delay in erecting the two pylons because of rough weather and as Mary Baker says, "The engineers found difficulty in convincing the London bosses that the wind could blow so fiercely and for days on end without ceasing." In September of that year the Falmouth Women's Institute had a request from the BBC to use their Hall to broadcast "Transatlantic Call" on the Forces programme; a sure sign that American forces were in the area in some strength.

The BBC also broadcast to the world, including occupied Europe, and many people there risked punishment tuning in to its wavelength to hear news they could trust. These broadcasts, from Bush House in London, often carried coded information after the evening news bulletins when personal messages were broadcast.. Ingenious systems were worked out to give advance warning to resistance fighters and agents of the time and the place for parachute drops.

In the build-up to Operation Overlord, as the invasion of Normandy was code-named, messages were worked out to first of all give the approximate time and then the precise time of invasion, so that acts of sabotage could be carried out behind the lines. The Germans had learnt some of these codes and on 5 June when they heard fifteen messages which they recognised as D-Day alerts, that Overlord was to happen that night, the commanders were warned. The message was passed to the 5th Army in the Calais area, where the invasion was expected, but it was not passed on to the troops of the 7th Army who were nearest the Normandy beaches.

The BBC was also preparing to announce to the country the momentous news of the invasion as soon as it had happened. Mary Baker and her colleague Phyllis Harding were on night duty at the Lanner transmitter at the beginning of June. Normally the transmitter was not powered at night but they would take it in turns to be awake in case of any important messages. This time they realised that something big was expected because each of them was told very firmly that during their four nights of work they both had to listen to the music programme from Plymouth for the whole night without a break. If a particular code word was broadcast they had to immediately power the Home Service transmitter to radiate vitally important news.

"I was told that if I disclosed anything to anybody about this the consequences would be very serious indeed. So we began our nights. Usually we took it in turns to doze but not now. There was a very big doormat at the entrance and we dragged it into a position alongside the Control Desk and lay down side-by-side on it. We plugged a pair of earphones into the Plymouth music line and turned the earpieces outwards so that with it between us we could both listen with one ear all the time. It was not very comfortable, but in case the discomfort was not enough to keep us awake, we told each other anything we could think of - favourite foods, black sheep in our families, rhymes, songs, jokes, anything to keep us awake. We heard nothing from Plymouth and were disappointed.

On the last morning, 6 June, when the day shift arrived and we had powered the transmitters as usual, we were all chatting together when we heard, "THIS IS LONDON" and then came the news that D-Day had arrived. We were all dumbstruck and shivering as we shook each others' hands."

At the Royal Cornwall Infirmary in Truro beds were being pulled away from the walls in preparation for ward cleaning. Marjory Jones wrote: "The man in the last bed still linked to the wall by his earphones heard:
'To the people of Western Europe. A landing was made on the coast of France by the Allied Expeditionary Force....'
'We're there. We've landed in France,' he shouted.
There was immediate reaction as those who were too weak called for nurses to push their beds back to listen. Others got out of bed and pushed for themselves. Nurses shared earphones with patients and over the faces of all there crept smiles of triumph."

16. D-DAY 6 JUNE 1944

"At the time of D-Day I was sitting on my own in the garden, and looked up to see the sky full of planes high overhead. I was quite stunned by this unusual sight, realised something big was happening and wondered how many of the men would return safely." So wrote Ivy Edwards of Perranarworthal. The "eerie silence" which had descended on Cornwall since the departure of the Americans was now shattered. Operation Overlord, the invasion of Normandy, was not just a huge amphibious operation but also one where air power played a vital part.

The first wave of bombers began the assault during the night of 5 June, trying to destroy the strongest coastal defences. These were followed by pathfinders marking out areas for the main airborne attack for troops landing by glider and parachute in the early hours of the morning to seize strategic points behind the beaches. In addition, planes covered large expanses of sea from the Irish coast to the south of Brittany dividing it into "corks", long, rectangular patrol areas, keeping a look out for E-boats, or U-boats surfacing to recharge their batteries. On that day there was no trouble as enemy craft had been confined to port because of the bad weather forecast, but in the ensuing days these planes, some from Predannack and St Eval, destroyed or damaged eleven U-boats and eliminated this potential threat.

Minesweepers were also busy on 5 June, clearing shipping lanes and marking them for the main invasion forces, and warships then moved in for a "softening up" process of shelling the coastal defences in the early hours of the morning. Bill Marshall, who had spent his childhood by the shores of Restronguet Creek near Devoran, was on board the destroyer, *HMS Saumerez*. Recently they had been on convoy duty in the cold and dangerous waters of the Arctic but in late May they had sailed south. On 3 June they were off Land's End waiting for orders, and now early on 6 June they were close to the Normandy coast ready for action. As he went to take up his position at the 4.7 gun he looked up to see the sky filled with hundreds of paratroopers floating down "like a snowstorm".

Deception was still important: the German belief that the main invasion would come near Calais had to be maintained to avoid reinforcements being sent into Normandy. Cyril Hart, a native of

Coverack, was with a small decoy fleet of MLs at Newhaven in Sussex at this time and he has written about his experiences.

"Troops began to arrive in Newhaven in thousands. The harbour was so crowded you could walk right across it from one landing craft to another. Eventually we moved outside the breakwater, our motor launch rolling in the swell to await further orders. The soldiers on board became very sick and didn't look much like assault troops. At last the orders came, but only to return to Newhaven. Another night in harbour, then off again. This time it was for real. We went, straight across the Channel, not by the route which had been cleared by the minesweepers.

"Our job that day was to approach the French coast well to the north of the invasion beaches and lure the Germans away from the main landing area. We knew that they had been monitoring our radio messages, so the wireless operators were given false messages to broadcast. We even had a Yankee sergeant put aboard at the last minute to give the impression that there were American ships as well as British ones. He was so ill that he read the script with his head over a bucket into which he spewed at frequent intervals. We also had a barrage balloon with a wire cage suspended below it, so constructed as to give the impression to a German radar operator of a large battleship approaching the coast. Other radar reflectors were mounted on special poles lashed to each side of the bridge.

"After a pretty rough crossing the three MLs of our group were approaching the French coast at about 4am Overhead were hundreds and hundreds of bombers going to blast the Channel fortifications. Suddenly the boat was lit up by a powerful beam. We fell flat on our faces expecting to hear bullets smacking into our wooden sides. Nothing happened. It was uncanny. Then we realised that just as we couldn't see the source of light, the searchlight operators couldn't see us. They were merely pointing the beam in the direction indicated by their radar. Soon we heard powerful engines racing towards us and a German destroyer appeared doing about 25 knots. We could only do 15 to 20. We made smoke which mingled with the morning mist and hoped it would work. It did. The destroyer must have picked up the reflections given off by the other MLs and thinking that a small fleet was approaching, dashed off towards the south. It was a relief and we continued our way towards the French coast.

"By now, the main invasion was in full swing to the south-west of us and when it was established that the Germans were forming up to repel what they thought was another attack by us, we were ordered to go back to Newhaven. We learned later that our ruse had caused several destroyers and E-boats and thousands of troops to be diverted from the beachheads where the actual landings were taking place and consequently our troops had been able to establish a foothold there."

Another young man on one of the "little ships" was Peter Waterfield, from Newtown-in-St Martin, on MTB 701 in the 63rd MTB "D" Class Flotilla. He was given the task of marking the ship's charts with top secret information giving the details of the cleared shipping lanes. He recalls, "I had to put all the details of this on our charts in the Ward Room with the door locked. If anyone came and tapped on the door, everything had to be folded and covered up before I was allowed to open the door." They left Portland at 6.00am on 5 June for Portsmouth to escort, with other similar craft, the spearhead of the assault convoys and minesweepers. "We went up the Solent between the Isle of Wight and the mainland. It was absolutely crammed, jammed tight with every sort of ship, but mainly landing craft of all descriptions. It was a truly amazing sight."

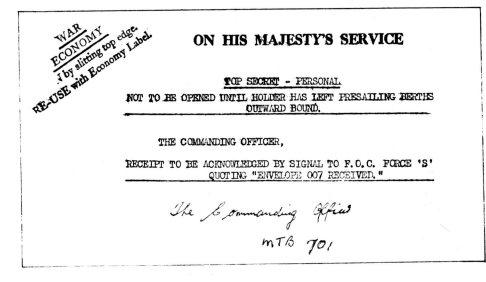

By dawn they were on the eastern flank of the invasion area off Le Havre. He recalls, "At about 5.30 the big ships began the bombardment and the destroyers moved close to the shore. I have a vivid picture of the dark shapes of the destroyers, slipping past a battleship, which was lobbing the shells right over. One destroyer hit a mine and broke in two forming a 'V' before it slipped down under the sea."

During the night all the invasion craft rendezvoused south of the Isle of Wight and then spread out to approach their designated beaches, the British Second Army making for the more eastern ones code-named Sword, Juno and Gold, while the United States First Army went further west towards the Cherbourg Peninsula to their invasion beaches, Omaha and Utah. The first landings were made here at 6.30am, with the British landing about an hour later, having decided to have a longer period of shelling of the coastal defences. By the end of the day all the beachheads had been gained, although not joined up as had been hoped, but the German Atlantic Wall had definitely been breached. Casualties at four of the beaches had been lighter than expected, but at Omaha there had nearly been complete disaster.

The initial assault here was made by the US V Corps, consisting of the 16th Infantry Combat Troop of the 1st Division, who had gained battle experience in North Africa, and the 116th Combat Troop of the 29th Division, whose experience had been gained only in exercises, mainly on Dartmoor and in other areas of the South-West. They were unfortunate to meet much sterner resistance than expected because the coastal forces had been strengthened by the German 352nd Infantry Division which was there on a full-scale practice. There were problems even before the American forces came close to the beach because of the rough seas.

Men gathered on the decks in the darkness; some climbed into their landing craft and were then lowered on to the waves; others had to clamber down nets over the side of the transporters to the smaller craft bucking up and down below them. Some were caught up in the mesh and dropped rifles and ammunition as they disentangled themselves. For two hours or more they had to endure choppy waves as they battled towards the unseen coast and sea sickness soon made the crowded boats almost unbearable.

Two or three hundred yards from the shore they came under heavy artillery fire. Water sprayed up around the boats as shells whistled past. Many were hit and burst into flames yards from the beach, littering the water with metal and bodies. Smoke filled their eyes and the roar of shells exploded in their ears as survivors tried to reach the shore. As the ramps of other boats crashed down on to the waves, men jumped into deep water and sank, weighed down by their heavy equipment. Many were hit as they floundered out of their depth, and drowning was just as much a threat as being shot. Some rid themselves of their encumbrances as quickly as possible. One Sergeant shed his heavy radio and assault jacket as mortar and artillery shells landed around him, then grabbing a log floating past with a mine attached, he pushed this in front of him as a shield to reach the beach.

Many of the DUKWS, swamped by waves, turned over and disappeared under the water, losing cannon, ammunition and sometimes men. Amphibious lorries carrying artillery capsized, and tanks were hit and set on fire as they reached the beach. Men floating in the water were strafed by machine-gun fire. They took shelter behind wreckage and dead bodies, and were in danger of being swept against small mines fixed to stakes near the sea edge. Some were in the water for an hour or more before they could crawl on to the beach with the rising tide, often without the weapons or ammunition to fight the enemy.

As more boats came in confusion increased. The only way to survive seemed to be to make for the cover of the sea wall on the far side of the wide beach. One officer was heard to say, "There are two kinds of soldiers on this beach. Those who are dead and those who are about to die. So let's get the hell off this damned beach."

This was easier said than done, not only because of the enemy defences and artillery fire but also because the Americans did not use any of the specialised tanks designed to clear mines and other obstacles. The beach was wide and protection was scant. Those who made it there found themselves pinned down in an inferno.

About one hour after the first landings eleven destroyers came close in to the beach and began to shell the German positions. They continued this intermittently through the day and slowly men began to climb up the low cliffs and make their way inland, away from the chaos of the beach strewn with bodies, equipment and wrecked vehicles.

About 10.30 that morning the 115th Combat Team, which had been based in the Bodmin area, formed part of the second wave that arrived at Omaha. There was still German opposition near the beach. Mortar and machine-gun fire was still creating havoc, and fires burned fiercely from tanks and fuel containers wrecked on the sands. Their orders to "pass through the 116th's initial objectives near the beach and take an objective near Longueville and strike out for St Lo," were obviously impossible to carry out, but they were eventually able to make their way inland to outflank the Germans holding up the first wave.

At a cost of over three thousand casualties a foothold had been gained here, mainly due to the determination of the infantrymen in the face of appalling odds. Major-General David Belchem writes in *Victory in Normandy*, "The day's fighting at Omaha had been a remarkable achievement by the US infantry and a great credit to the skilful action of the warships supporting them." But as one officer wrote, "Why do these things have to be forced upon men?"

D-Day 6 June 1944

On the other beaches the initial landings had been easier and beachheads had been gained more quickly and with fewer casualties. However at Juno, where Canadian forces landed without too much difficulty, in spite of reefs and bad weather conditions, there were great losses as the landing craft withdrew from the beach. Captain Dan Flunder, who now lives in Manaccan, was adjutant of 48 Commando which landed there. He writes, "The sea was covered with craft as far as the eye could see. The shore was under bombardment, craft were sinking, and from where I stood it certainly didn't look as if the Canadians had secured the beach - things didn't look good at all......The beach was covered in casualties, some Canadians, some ours. The surf was incredible, with beached and half-sunken craft wallowing about in it.....Some tanks struggled ashore and some bogged in the shingle......I was sickened to see one run over two of our wounded...." In spite of all the difficulties the Canadians penetrated farther inland than any other Allied formation on D-Day.

However, this was only the start of the campaign in Normandy. Many more men, vehicles and weapons were needed to consolidate the initial successes. Some were already on their way and would soon be pouring on to these hard-won beaches.

17. THE END IN SIGHT

When Pilot Officer Wichelo reported for duty at St Athan near Cardiff, on Tuesday 6 June, D-Day, he was given escort duty for vessels leaving Barry Docks, flying his Anson aircraft at 2,000 feet keeping a look-out for U-boats. He recalls picking up two ships "which looked like barges with great tarpaulins over them." He flew down to take a closer look. "All of a sudden the tarpaulins went back and there were hundreds of faces looking up at us. We dropped right down and flew alongside them; they raised their hats and waved." These men might well have been some of the 29th Division, which had been stationed in the South-West, departing for Omaha Beach in support of the men who had landed earlier. It was only after seeing them that the airmen realised what must be happening. "We tuned into the BBC and heard on the News that our first troops had gone ashore, so we knew it was D-Day."

The 110th Field Artillery, which had embarked on the St Germans River in five British LCTs on 4 June, were also landing at Omaha in support of the assault troops, on D-Day plus 1. They left Plymouth in a large convoy screened by battleships, cruisers and destroyers. Each craft held one battery consisting of four 105mm guns, lorries, ammunition and one hundred and five men, all so packed in that movement was very limited, and they remained in these cramped conditions for three days because of the twenty-four hour postponement. During this time they were on cold rations supplemented by the occasional cup of hot coffee, and celery soup from self-heating tins. "I never want another can of celery soup," says Wire Corporal Michael Crawford.

When they approached the beach they saw it was littered with battle detritus, including a US destroyer escort washed up on the beach by the surf during the close bombardment of the German batteries the previous day. No German guns were strafing the beach now but at the start of the day it had still been covered by German artillery fire. Directed by the beachmaster with a tannoy and a "bulldog on a leash" they were able to land without getting wet and Michael Crawford drove his Wire Jeep straight across the beach and on to the town of Vierville, where the 29th Division was held up. "There were wounded everywhere, tanks burnt out, vehicles of all descriptions wrecked and debris scattered everywhere. War was all around us. It was not like Okehampton."

They joined up with the 115th Combat Troops, which had landed the previous day, in an area infested by snipers. "They were everywhere, church steeples, hedgerows and houses." The first enemy to surrender to them, hands held high above his head, was "Chinese-looking", later identified as a Mongolian. "He stood there with a silly grin on his face with big buck teeth. Then more guys popped up from other foxholes with their hands in the air. They were all the same. They were very short, had no uniform, just a sackcloth coat......Apparently they were captured by the Germans on the Russian front and had been forced into the German army as cannon fodder on the Atlantic Wall."

That evening the 63rd MTB Flotilla patrolling off Omaha Beach, received an emergency order to go to the help of a hospital ship that had been mined. They found three ships which had strayed beyond the cleared lanes, one undamaged which they escorted back to safer waters, and two damaged but not in immediate danger of sinking. These were the *Dinard* and the *St Julien*, both of which had called into Falmouth Harbour in April for fuel at the time when vessels were beginning to gather for the invasion. The hospitals, recently cleared of civilian patients, would soon be seeing the results of the opening of the Second Front.

Cyril Hart, who had been with the decoy fleet early in the morning of D-Day, found himself crossing the Channel on the following day in an Infantry Landing Craft, transporting Canadian troops to Juno Beach. Each man had a bicycle so that after landing they could circle behind the enemy to attack from the rear. As they approached the beach they passed merchant ships unloading stores and ammunition into landing craft, and then the battleship, *Ansen*, firing salvoes at targets beyond the beach. Just as they were dropping anchor a buzz bomb "came careering down the beach. It seemed to be making straight for us. Fortunately it landed in the sea astern."

The beach was covered with landing craft, vehicles, stores, ammunition boxes and bodies. "It was ordered confusion. Everyone seemed to know what he was doing and took no notice of what anyone else was doing." Some of the craft were not familiar: there was an LCR (Landing Craft Rocket) manned by marines. "It could deliver a salvo more deadly than that of a battle cruiser." There was also a LCK (Landing Craft Kitchen) which landed tanks but was also fitted with galleys, "bristling with chimneys shaped like a letter 'H' on a stick", to provide hot meals for the men on the beach.

As they lowered the ramps, the Canadians "dashed down into the sea which came up to their chests. They carried their bikes on their heads and several went flat on their faces and were wet through before they reached dry land." Within minutes they had finished unloading and were ready to return to Portsmouth, but they found themselves stuck there, under intermittent attack, with the propeller jammed round with wire. "I can still remember the sound of shells coming over like a train going through a tunnel," writes Cyril Hart. "I've tried to forget the sound of screams as a man is dying of horrible burns and one can do nothing to help. I remember being so tired that I lay down and went to sleep and woke up during an air attack. I shook the sailor next to me and found that he was dead."

He later returned on another vessel carrying German prisoners stinking from days of fighting, lying in ditches, hiding in cattle sheds and crawling through mud. "When they got into the hold, the steam started rising and the smell was indescribable." Four years earlier it had been the British soldiers returning from defeat in France who were tired, dirty and smelly.

Meanwhile the 63rd MGB Flotilla, with Peter Waterfield, was still continuing its patrols off Omaha Beach, but by now the greatest necessity seemed to be to find fuel, food and water for themselves. They found one ship which could supply them with some stores, and later tied up to a merchant vessel near a Mulberry Harbour component. "There were black US troops waiting to go ashore and one of them tried to throw a bar of chocolate to one of our men, but it fell in the water. Soon they were all throwing their chocolate, probably their emergency rations for the next few days. Nearly all of it landed in the sea, but it was a fine gesture of generosity. I will always remember those fine people."

At the Helford River the following day the SIS contingent, including John Garnett, received orders to report to Portsmouth in one of their French fishing boats. They were then told to join a convoy going across to Courseulles, by Juno Beach, to carry members of the SIS who were to reconnoitre the situation for passing agents through this beachhead. They set out for the marshalling area south of the Isle of Wight, "Piccadilly Circus", where all the ships came in from the ports of the south coast to follow the cleared lanes to the beaches, and arrived at Juno on Saturday morning 10 June. There they moored behind the "Gooseberry", old ships sunk to give protection to the beach. John Garnett was eating a meal the following day in Bayeux at the Lion d'Or, which on Tuesday 6 June had been serving German officers and two days later had been welcoming Allied forces.

They returned to Portsmouth to fetch another fishing boat to act as a reception boat for agents brought over by MGBs. Shortly after their return to France they experienced terrible gales which caused great damage. These storms badly delayed the landing of much-needed ammunition and other supplies and on one of these days, when the situation seemed particularly gloomy, John Garnett had a memorable meeting on the beach.

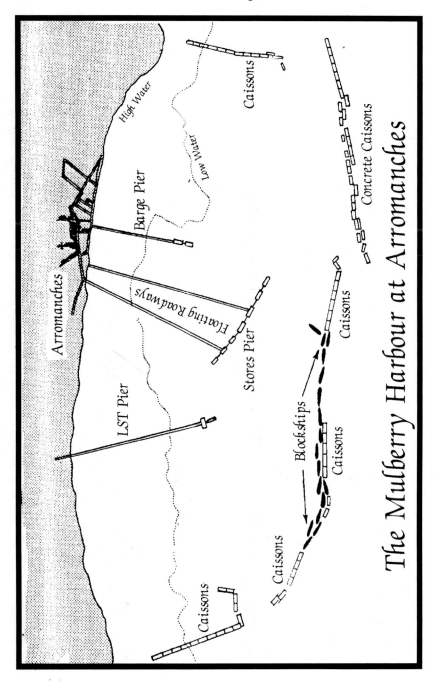

The Mulberry Harbour at Arromanches

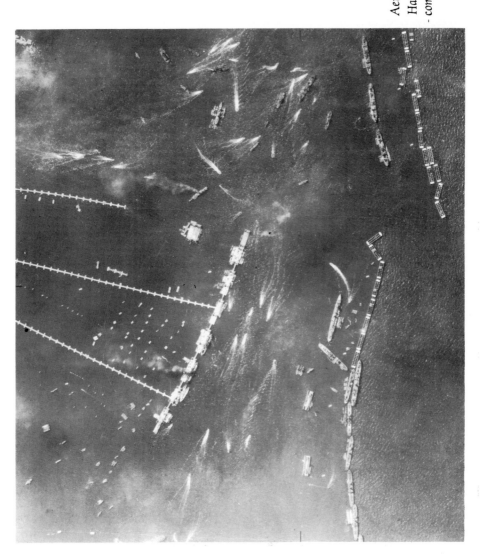

Aerial view of Mulberry Harbour at Arromanches - compare with map above. (P. Waterfield)

The End in Sight

"Who should be coming along the beach but a small man with a beret, accompanied by two staff officers - there was General Montgomery himself. What that did for the morale of people there was simply staggering. Until then, being a sailor, I had always thought of him as a bit of a 'bull-shitter', but there he was with us, right up where the front line was, and we knew then that it was going to be all right."

The storms that hit the Channel on 19 June did not die down for nearly four days and were the worst for forty years. Total disaster on the beaches was averted only by the "Gooseberry" breakwaters which broke up the force of the waves. During the worst of the storm, unloading came to a stop. In the three preceding days nineteen thousand men and three thousand vehicles had been landed at Omaha and Utah beaches. Between the 19th and 22nd only six thousand men and one thousand vehicles were brought ashore.

On two of the beaches, Gold in the British sector and Omaha in the American area, the breakwaters were enlarged to form the Mulberry Harbours. Inside the protective barrier three floating piers were planned, linked to the shore by floating roadways. More than two hundred caissons were towed across the Channel, some of them the size of five-storey buildings. Unfortunately the storm damaged the two piers already being built at Omaha and they were completely written off, but the building of the British Mulberry was further advanced. Although there was damage, the piers were able to be used, but unloading did not begin again until 29 June and the final pier was not operative until the end of July. It remained in use until November playing a vital part in the supplying of the army, as the French ports were temporarily put out of action by the Germans.

Falmouth had become a forward base for the operations at Arromanches, Gold Beach. Craft damaged by the storm were brought here for repair and floating pier heads came in from the remote ports where they had been built, to be tested in great secrecy mainly near St Mawes. These pierheads were about two hundred feet long by sixty feet wide, with a massive steel leg at each corner. These could be raised or lowered separately so that the whole structure could stand firmly on the sea bed.

Lieutenant Ludlum, a Sapper in the Port Artisan Company, Royal Engineers, arrived at the end of June "on a glorious day, the sea and the sky a deep blue." He was on one of these pier heads, damaged by German guns, being towed into the Bay for major repair work to be done at the Docks. Two Falmouth tugs took up the towing "resplendent in peace time colours and gleaming brass work," and took them around the Castle headland and into the Helford River, where they moored near the SIS yacht *Sunbeam*. "Going in was like leaving the war outside. We felt safe after our hazardous voyage."

Mulberry Harbour component on the Helford (M. Collins)

During these days in June many US merchant vessels arrived in Falmouth to load at the Docks, some making regular visits and establishing a shuttle service between Cornwall and Normandy. Many of these must have brought back wounded soldiers. In later weeks when the hectic activity was dying down the *Fort Bedford* came in to harbour with hundreds of wounded on board. The ship was in such a dirty state that the dockers refused to clean her out. Hundreds of soiled and stinking mattresses had to be loaded into railway wagons to be taken away for burning, and this unpleasant task was the last job undertaken by Lieutenant Ludlum and other Royal Engineers before they left Falmouth. "We marched off the old *Fort Bedford* - our last Falmouth ship - needing a good wash all round but with a bad job well done."

By the end of June the Allied Forces had not yet broken through the German defences in Normandy. On 23 June the 5th Battalion of the Duke of Cornwall's Light Infantry arrived in Normandy as part of the 43rd (Wessex) Division and were soon involved in fierce fighting at Hill 112, for which they gained battle honours. This was part of Operation Epsom in the advance on Caen and has been described as "probably the most decisive battle of the entire campaign." In early July the town was bombed and taken, when John Garnett at Juno Beach saw the sky filled with four-engined bombers.

The 776th Anti-Aircraft Weapons Battalion, based at Trelissick, was still there ready to defend Falmouth against the chance of retaliatory attacks, but some of the batteries were moved to Fowey and Plymouth, also important ports for the operations across the Channel. They were expecting to be sent to the other side in August but "without warning the battalion was notified on the 14 July that it could consider Trelissick House its concentration area for preparation for movement to the continent. The next day, after a night of feverish packing, the batteries moved to the marshalling area near Chacewater." Two days later they were embarking at Falmouth on two of the "shuttle" boats, the SS *William N Pendleton* and the SS *Edwin S Abbey*.

Both these liberty ships were "dirty from top to bottom", and it was difficult to keep clean for more than an hour. On board the SS *William N Pendleton* living conditions were cramped as well as filthy. "More than 500 men, including part of a Negro quartermaster outfit and part of a battalion of White camouflage engineers, were all jammed down in one hold. Even the officers were in the hold."

To add to their troubles they spent much longer aboard than planned. First of all fog settled down over the convoy. "The fog horns started blowing and kept it up at regular intervals. The two ships carrying men of the 776th battalion stayed with the huge convoy until Cherbourg harbor was reached and then broke off and sailed along the coast to their destination, Omaha Beach." The men were not allowed on shore until all the equipment had been unloaded and this operation was delayed because of storms. When they finally set foot on French soil it was not until 23 July.

The break-out from Normandy had not yet been achieved and they "witnessed the spectacle of a huge fleet of bombers converge on St Lo, only a few miles away, and dump their bombs on that doomed city. They saw the dive-bombers come in first. And then they saw the heavies. Hundreds of them flew relentlessly towards St Lo. And behind them, in a seemingly never-ending stream, came hundreds more. It was an awe-inspiring sight, and one that most of the men will never forget."

In due course the break-through was achieved and this battalion, like many others, reached the River Rhine. Victory in Europe was in sight. Never again would such huge concourses of ships be seen in Falmouth Bay as in those June days of 1940 and 1944, when Cornwall first welcomed exhausted troops and refugees into a county preparing to repel the threatened invasion, and then four years later witnessed the departure of part of the greatest armada in the history of the world.

BIBLIOGRAPHY

Barnett C.   1991   *Engage the Enemy More Closely* Hodder and Stoughton
Balkowski J.   1989   *Beyond the Beachhead* Stackpole
Belchem D.   1981   *Victory in Normandy* Chatto and Windus
Breakell B.   1990   *Falmouth at War* Amigo Books
Colville J.   *The Fringes of Power* Hodder & Stoughton
Cooper J.P.   *The History of the 110th Field Artillery* Maryland Historical
          Society
Dorman J.   1990   *The Later Defences of Falmouth* Ravelin
Ewing J.H.   1948   *29 Let's Go* Infantry Journal Press Washington
Edwards I.   1988   *The Family at Rose Villa*
Essame H.   1951   *The 43rd Wessex Division at War* Clowes
Foot M.R.D.   1984   *S.O.E. Special Operations Executive*   BBC
Freeman R.   1984   *Mighty Eighth War Manual* Jane's
Gedenboek   *Enys House 1940-46* Het Koninklijk Instituut voor de Marine
Gerrard J.   1982   *The Book of Plymouth* Barracuda
Gilbert M.   1986   *The Road to Victory* Heinemann
Gilson P.   1990   *Falmouth in Old Photographs* Alan Sutton Publ. Ltd.
Gloux H.   1976   *Les Bateaux de Peche de Bretagne* Fayard
Hart C.S.   1990   *Cornish Oasis* The Lizard Press
Hastings M. 1984   *Overlord* Michael Joseph
Hichens R.   1943   *We Fought Them in Gunboats*
The History of the 776th Anti-Aircraft Battalion
Hoyte E.P.   1987   *The Invasion Before Normandy* Robert Hale
Jones R.V.   1978   *Most Secret War* Hamish Hamilton
Lampe D.   1968   *The Last Ditch* Cassell
Low S.   1971   *Jane's Fighting Ships* Marston & Co
Moulton J.L. 1963   *Haste to the Battle* Cassell
Neillands R. 1987   *By Sea and Land* Weidenfeld and Nicholson
Longmate N. 1975   *The GIs The Americans in Britain 1942-5* Hutchinson
Phillips C.E.L.   *The Greatest Raid of All* Companion Book Club
Poole Historical Trust 1980   *Poole and World War Two*
Rabey I.   *Cornwall's Fire Brigade* Ivan Rabey
Schenk P.   1990   *The Invasion of England* Conway
Smith G.   *When Jim Crow Met John Bull* I.B.Tauris & Co. Ltd
Rendell J.   1993   *Launceston - Some Pages in History* Landfall Publications
Tangye N.   1981   *Cornwall and the Tumbling Sea* William Kimber

(Various) 1993   *D-Day Operation Overlord* Salamander
(Various) 1989   *The World at Arms* Readers Digest
Walford E.   1989   *War Over the West* Amigo Books
West N.   1992   *Secret War* Hodder and Stoughton
Wickstead B.   *Father's Heinkel*
Williams M.   *My Island War* Own Press
Young P.   1981   *D-Day* Bison Books Ltd.

INDEX
Photographs in italics

St Mawes 13, 43, 70, 74, 97, 115-6, 158
St Keverne 23, 50, *51*, 52, 111
SIS (Secret Intelligence Service) & SOE (Secret Operations Executive) 55-68,
     56-7, 60, 61, 64-8, 155
Slapton Sands 119, 121, 123
SOE See SIS above
Swanvale 21, 52, *126*, 127, 130

Trebah 97, 104, 108-9, 111, *112, 113,* 113-4, 130, 132, 138-141, *140*
Tregildry Guest House 39, 130
Trelan 34, 70
Trelawny, Ian 74
Trelissick 99, 101, 123, 134, 160
Trefusis 92
Tolverne 46, 109, 113-4, 123, 140-1
Truro 26, 33, 35, 37, 46, 54, 82, 86-8, *91*, 92, 96, 101, 103, 105, 114, 138, 146
Torpoint 21, 96, 101, 137-8, 141
Turnaware 46, 109, 111, 113, 119, 132, 134, 140-1

US Army, 29th Division 95-6, 99, 116, 118-9, *120-2*, 121, 132, 137-8, *140*, 141,
     142, 143, 150, 151, 160
US Navy (see under Falmouth)

Warington Smyth, Bevil & Nigel 63
Women's Institute (WI) 20, 82, 99, 108, 145
Women's Land Army 90-2, *91*
Women's Voluntary Service (WVS) 18, 20-21, 25, 52, 82-4, 96

BY THE SAME AUTHORS
The Sequel to
OPERATION CORNWALL

CORNISH WAR & PEACE
The Road to Victory - and Beyond

Cornish War & Peace is a sequel to *Operation Cornwall 1940-1944* in two ways. First of all it gives more details on some of the topics discussed in the earlier book as well as dealing with several aspects of the war in Cornwall scarcely mentioned before. Secondly it goes on to the end of the war, to the victory celebrations and the immediate aftermath.

It seems clear that the Second World War, either directly or indirectly, brought great changes to Cornwall. Cornish people found themselves in parts of the world they would never normally have expected to see, and strangers arrived in Cornwall who would scarcely have heard of it before. The Duchy suddenly assumed strategic importance, which is still shown today by the largest naval helicopter base in the county, as well as by a variety of communication systems on cliffs, downs and beaches.

CONTENTS
Tolverne - "Down at the Ferry Boat Inn" - Men Who Dared Death - The Christmas Rescue - Women at War - Lines around the World   (Cable & Wireless at Porthcurno) - Radar, the Secret Weapon - "The Eyes and Ears of All Our Defences" (Royal Observer Corps) - Cornish Airfields - Victory and Peace, 1945 - Victory in Europe - A Bitter Hand to Hand Campaign - Leonard Cheshire - Wild Goose, Swallow and Nerve Gas (Airfields after the War, with special emphasis on the work of Barnes Wallis) - "Now Win the Peace" -   Problems of Peace - Optimism for the Future POSTSCRIPT: The Festival of Britain APPENDIX 1. The Tragedy of the *Lancastria* 2. Special Construction 3. American Forces & D-Day 4. The Return of the *Mutin* 5. The Secret Army 6. The Lavatory before the Flush - BIBLIOGRAPHY - INDEX

168 pages, fully illustrated, thread-sewn paperback, price £6.99

LANDFALL PUBLICATIONS

Also by Viv Acton
LIFE BY THE FAL
Years of Change at Point and Penpol
A detailed study of a small waterside community near Devoran that was caught up in Cornwall's Industrial Revolution. Liberally illustrated with sketches and photographs, many in colour. Price: £4.95

HIGH DAYS: Truro High School Celebrates
Published in 1996 to mark the centenary of the present buildings on Falmouth Road. Price: £3.00

A HISTORY OF TRURO
Volume 1: From Coinage Town to Cathedral City
A very readable and fully illustrated history. Price: £8.25 paperback, £12.00 hardback

Explore the places that feature in OPERATION CORNWALL in the most enjoyable way - ON FOOT!
Bob Acton's LANDFALL WALKS BOOKS
provide detailed directions plus lots of background information for round walks in the following areas:
The Fal, Helford and Fowey estuaries - The north coast of Cornwall from Padstow almost to Land's End - Most of the south coast from Penzance to Looe - Many inland areas including those around Truro, Camborne, Redruth, Liskeard, Lostwithiel and St Austell.
The books include sketch maps and are fully illustrated with sketches and photographs. Prices range from £1.25 to £4.95.

OTHER LANDFALL BOOKS
Exploring Cornwall's Tramway Trails *(Bob Acton) 2 vols, £6.99 each*
Exploring Cornish Mines *(Kenneth Brown & Bob Acton)*
(4 volumes so far, various prices)
The Bells of Truro *(Phyllis Jones) £4.95*
St Ives Heritage *(Lena & Donald Bray) £5.99*
Newquay's Pictorial Past *£3.00*
Launceston: Some Pages in History *(Joan Rendell) £9.99*
"To Clothe the Fields with Plenty" *(John & Pat Hanson) £3.99*

The books are available from local shops and direct from the publisher. Mail orders: please add 20% for postage, up to a maximum of £5.